SPECIAL NEEDS IN MAINSTREAM SCHOOLS

Series Editor: Keith Postlethwaite

# CLASSROOM RESPONSES TO DISRUPTIVE BEHAVIOUR

James Gray and John Richer

ROUTLEDGE

First published 1988 by Macmillan Education Ltd
Reprinted 1989, 1990, 1991

Reprinted by Routledge 1992
11 New Fetter Lane, London EC4P 4EE

*British Library Cataloguing in Publication Data*

**ISBN** 0-415-08428-8

A catalogue reference for this title is available
from the British Library.

Printed and bound in Hong Kong by
Dah Hua Printing Press.

# Contents

**8**

**9**

# Preface

This book, and its companion volumes, are intended for teachers and student teachers interested in mainstream secondary education. This volume deals with responses which an individual teacher can make, in his or her own classroom, to the problem of pupils whose behaviour is disruptive. The other volumes deal with classroom responses to learning difficulties and with the organisational response.of the whole school to that fifth of its pupils who have special educational needs.

The approach taken in the series is based on the idea that special needs can only be adequately met in schools if all teachers recognise that they have a role to play, and if all are able to develop some appropriate skills. This starting point does not negate the importance of specialist provision from special needs departments – indeed much of the volume on organisational responses deals specifically with how such departments might be organised. However, we do firmly believe that without an element of response from every teacher there are severe limitations on what a special needs department can achieve.

In this book we concentrate on the issue of disruptive behaviour. The aim is to help mainstream teachers improve their understanding of the problem and to extend the range of strategies which they can use in their own classrooms to avoid disruption as far as possible, and to deal with it when it occurs.

The general approach of the book is a practical one, with suggestions for activities which a teacher might do. To draw attention to these activities we have used a tinted background, with an **A** in the margin. We also occasionally summarise a set of ideas or emphasise a key point by placing text between heavy horizontal lines, with an **i** in the margin.

We hope the book will be useful to individual teachers or students working on their own, to groups following formal pre-service and in-service training courses and to ad hoc groups that might come together in individual schools to explore, as a group of colleagues, some of the most demanding tasks which we have to undertake as teachers.

K.C.P.
Oxford 1986

# **A**cknowledgements

This book owes a great deal to many people who have contributed ideas of their own and discussed our ideas with us. In particular we would like to thank Michael Argyle, Claudia Beamish, Ann Hackney, Roy Howarth, Mike Kent and Keith Postlethwaite.

Much useful comment was also provided by representatives from each of the University Departments of Education in England and Wales who met in London and in Oxford to discuss our research programme in general, and draft versions of these materials in particular.

Our colleagues in the Oxford Department of Educational Studies have given us much helpful advice, and some have tried out a number of the activities with their own students. In particular we would like to thank Elizabeth Hitchfield for her constructive comments on the text and for her general support.

We are also indebted to all the PGCE students in Oxford over the past three years who experienced earlier versions of the text and provided us with useful feedback.

Finally we would like to thank Elizabeth Paren, our editor at Macmillan, for her help in bringing the book to completion.

# Introduction

If you want to learn something about classroom disruption, the following is an interesting exercise.

Go into any school, and find out the name of a pupil whose behaviour is really worrying the staff. Then go into the staff-room, and ask the teachers the following two questions:

**1.** Why is the pupil so disruptive?
**2.** What can be done about the problem?

These two questions can really open up the whole topic. You can also make two very good bets about answers to these two questions.

First you will probably get almost as many different answers as you have interviewees. In other words, teachers do not generally agree about disruptive pupils, in terms of either the causes of the behaviour, or the solutions that should be implemented.

The second bet is that a high proportion of the answers will identify causes and solutions outside the competences of the interviewee.

So, saying that the behaviour is caused, for instance, by the parents does not point the teacher towards any kind of solution that he or she can implement. Debating the relative importance of the attitudes of society to schooling and the effects of the exam system will also fail to offer an accessible solution to a teacher. Saying that the child needs special help, or should be in a special school probably won't help either, because such provision is scarce, and is generally being decreased because of recent legislations.

Both these bets sound cynical and insulting to teachers; they are not meant to be. They really highlight the teacher's dilemma over disruptive behaviour. On the one hand teachers are confronted daily with disruptive behaviour in their classes and it is clearly of great significance to them. At the very least it interferes with their teaching; more probably it makes them feel incompetent and inadequate. On the other hand teachers are told that the causes of the problem lie in areas to which they as teachers do not have access; the child's family and personality, the school's structure or their own tendency to characterise people in terms of their behaviour.

This book is intended to address these twin problems of understanding the causes of disruption and effecting solutions.

---

The first part reviews some of the findings in the literature and offers an understanding of disruptive behaviour which involves the teacher as a central actor. Such an understanding necessarily underlies appropriate classroom responses. This part should not, therefore, be overlooked.

The second part is drawn from this understanding and offers practical recommendations to teachers. These can be regarded as specific recipes, but the intention is that they should be seen more as examples that illustrate the underlying idea and theory.

---

# Part 1   Understanding disruption

# How big is the problem?

In the caricature staff-room described in the introduction, another scene is commonly observed (or experienced). A harassed teacher slumps in during break and confesses: 'I don't know what to do with Michael in 3c. He just destroyed my lesson.'

The reply comes back: 'Oh! He's no trouble with me.'

A response like that can mean a range of things, but is hardly likely to make our harassed teacher feel better, or fare better with Michael on Thursday. However, something can be gleaned from this conversation.

First, our harassed teacher is likely to be left with the impression, not only of being incompetent, but also of being the only incompetent teacher around. How realistic is his fear of being the only teacher who finds disruption to be a problem? This was investigated by Dierenfield (1982) who, from a questionnaire to teachers, established that only 8 per cent of his respondents felt that disruption was *not* really a problem; the remaining 92 per cent felt that it was a problem, although most (68 per cent) felt that it was possible to cope with it.

These figures should be some consolation to our imaginary teacher but they should not produce complacency. A class repeatedly punctuated by disruptive incidents is not one in which a curriculum, however carefully devised, can be well pursued. Even pupils, contrary perhaps to popular conception, seem to want lessons to be free from disruption. They certainly rank as the most important characteristic of a teacher, the ability to control the class (Gannaway 1976).

We can conclude that disruption is commonly seen as a problem, and as a problem that matters.

A second point which can be drawn from our imaginary staff-room conversation is that it is not easy to assess the incidence of disruption in any objective terms. In attempts to do so, several definitions of disruption have been used. Most assessments have determined the numbers of individual pupils whose behaviour has had certain *consequences*. For example, Galloway *et al.*, (1982) determined the incidence of *suspension from school*, and came up with a figure of 0.001 per cent of the school population. Dawson (1982) on the other hand used the criterion of causing an *'unusually high degree of concern for behavioural reasons'* to the pupil's teachers as his definition, and found a rate of 1.5 per cent of pupils.

Assessments such as these of the incidence of disruption tend to overlook the third point to be made about the staff-room conversation. It is perfectly possible that the pupil who disrupted one teacher's lesson to the point of destruction, really did not disrupt the other teacher's lessons. In other words, the identification of a disruptive pupil emerges from interactions between teacher and pupil – the disruption is a part of that relationship. Pupils are not disruptive in vacuo. At any one moment they may disrupt a particular lesson, with a particular teacher (a consideration that occupies most of this book).

The definition used by one of the present authors in a study of disruption conducted for the Oxford Educational Research Group followed these considerations. It embraced the idea that disruption occurs as part of a relationship and therefore accepted the nominations by the participants in the relationships – teachers and pupils – to identify individuals who disrupted lessons.

Thus all the staff teaching the third year (ages 13–14 years) in two comprehensive schools in Oxfordshire were asked to name pupils who disrupted their lessons. 7.3 per cent (26) pupils were nominated by two or more teachers (the criterion of more than one teacher was used to avoid idiosyncratic relationship problems when identifying pupils themselves as disruptive).

All third year pupils were themselves asked to nominate disruptive pupils. 27 per cent (97) received two or more nominations. The same prevalence rate (about 7 per cent) identified by two teachers was achieved by a cut off point of 10 or more pupil nominations. This produced 7.6 per cent (27) pupils identified as disruptive.

All such cut off points (in this case 2+ teachers, 10+ pupils) are to some extent arbitrary. However the validity of these cut off points was shown by comparing the pupil and teacher nominations. To a great extent they identified the same pupils. This coincidence of identification was high and significant, suggesting that nominations reflect more than simply idiosyncratic relationship problems. 5.1 per cent of pupils were jointly identified as disruptive by 2 or more teachers *and* 10 or more pupils. It is also important to note that the overwhelming majority of those identified as disruptive were boys. For this reason, disruptive pupils will be referred to in this book as 'he'. This in no way denies that girls can be a serious problem, and the differences between disruptive boys and girls will be considered in Chapter 9.

This incidence rate of 5 per cent was from schools without bad reputations and in a medium size county town in which rates would be expected to be low. This figure is likely to represent the lower end of the incidence range (deprived inner city areas are likely to have greater incidence (cf Rutter *et al.*, 1979)). It suggests that in an average secondary school class of 30 pupils, at least one or two of them will be generally identified as disruptive.

These findings should be some consolation to our imaginary teacher in the staff-room, indeed to any teacher whose lessons have been disrupted. You are not alone. Classroom disruption is clearly a very common phenomenon. It involves far more pupils than would ever be considered as candidates for referral to special schools, and far more than would be the subject of formal assessment under the Education Act, 1981. It is a phenomenon with very far-reaching effects. However it is a problem that teachers can do something about and for this reason it is extremely important that teachers should know more about it, should do something about it and reduce the problem.

To reduce the incidence of disruption in classrooms requires an understanding of the phenomenon. Such an understanding can be gained by starting from two separate points. The first of these is the background to the phenomenon. Disruption is not a random phenomenon, and a great deal can be learned about it by studying the situations in which it occurs, and the backgrounds of those most frequently involved. This will be discussed in Chapter 2.

The second starting point is implicit in the use of subjective identifications of disruptive individuals in the Oxford Study. This underlines the fact that disruptive behaviour is essentially interactive and so emphasises the necessity to consider the behaviour of all those involved, both teachers and pupils. This will be considered in Chapter 3.

# The background to disruption

## 2.1 Disruptive pupils – Disruptive incidents

In considering the background to disruption it is essential to bear in mind one outstanding point. To talk about 'a disruptive pupil' is a shorthand, and some authors (particularly Hargreaves *et al.,* 1975) have stressed that it is a dangerous shorthand. It is *disruptive incidents* that have to be considered, and it is important to do so if only to avoid the pernicious effects of labelling the *pupil* as disruptive. These effects can include using the label in a wide range of circumstances when the pupil may only be involved in disruptive incidents in a particular set of circumstances; using the label beyond the time for which it is valid (and therefore ignoring the possibility that pupils can change); ignoring the interactive nature of disruption by putting all the blame on the pupil.

*A very easy trap to fall into.*

These dangers and consequences have been discussed at length by Hargreaves *et al.* (op.cit.) and will be considered further in Chapter 4. Having given warning about the term 'disruptive pupil', two things have to be said. First, it is a normal tendency to generalise from experiencing that a person does such-and-such to thinking of that person as a 'such-and-such person'. This applies whether they are clever, rude, aggressive or warm; the normal tendency is to apply the label – to generalise from observed behaviour to using the term as a description of the person (Hargreaves *et al.,* op.cit.).

The other point to be made about the shorthand phrase 'disruptive pupil' is that it does correspond to observable facts to some extent. In Chapter 1 the coincidence of identification of disruptive pupils as between teachers and pupils was noted, and the inference is that certain pupils are involved in disruptive incidents more frequently than others. It is clear that there are pupils who are frequently disruptive with many teachers and in many school contexts (Galloway *et al.,* 1982) and over a long period (Farrington, 1978). It seems that the use of shorthand labels is not without foundation. Similarly there are teachers who suffer above average disruption (Hargreaves *et al.,* op.cit., Marsh *et al.,* 1978).

## 2.2 Explanations of disruption

Explanations of disruption have been offered at several different levels. So, at the broadest level, disruption has been related to the unemployment rate,

(Raven, 1979), and to the contrast between the raised school-leaving age and the ever lowering age of puberty (Frude, 1984).

Such factors are remote from the school and while a teacher is wise to bear them in mind they do not explain why one pupil or one school is repeatedly involved in disruption when others are not. Investigation at this more individual level throws a great deal of light on the problem. A general and increasingly familiar picture emerges of the background characteristics of these pupils, their schools and their home contexts.

*But why are a minority of pupils disruptive?*

The disruptive pupils as a group tend to have lower IQ, poor academic attainment, lower socio-economic class, a relatively high prevalence of 'neurological' problems, to come from broken homes or homes where there is marital discord, and from families with financial or housing difficulties, they tend to suffer harsh and/or inconsistent discipline at home from fathers who may have a criminal or psychiatric history (Shephard *et al.*, 1971; Rutter *et al.*, 1975; Farrington, 1978; Graham and Rutter, 1968; Galloway *et al.*, 1982; Sturge, 1983; Frude, 1984).

*Interactive nature of disruption*

In addition, schools differ in their rates of disruption and delinquency more than the characteristics of their pupil intake would predict (Power *et al.*, 1967; Rutter *et al.*, 1979; Galloway, 1980). This emphasises the interactive nature of the problem. Some of the factors of school organisation and ethos which correlate with *low* rates of disruption/delinquency are: emphasis on reward rather than punishment, immediacy of action on indiscipline, turning a blind eye to some rule breaking, not encroaching on pupils out-of-school activities, teachers being approachable about pupils' personal problems, involving pupils in leadership activities, punctuality of teachers, well prepared lessons, a democratic organisation of teachers (Power, 1972; Reynolds, 1975; Rutter *et al.*, 1979; Frude, 1984).

In our own study disruptive pupils were found to differ in many ways from non-disruptive pupils. Part of the study was done in the third year (age 13 to 14) in two schools. A self completion questionnaire was given to all the pupils in the year group. The results were factor analysed and two factors, 'social skills with adults' and 'academic self-image' emerged which distinguished disruptive from non-disruptive pupils. Disruptive pupils scored low on social skills with adults and had low academic self-images.

'Social skills' is the term developed (see for instance Argyle, 1978) to describe an individual's competence at relating to other people. 'Social skills with adults' refers to the capacity of a young person to relate to adults successfully. Having low social skills with adults suggests that disruptive pupils are unlikely to achieve their goals in dealings with adults, producing instead feelings of anger, annoyance or dislike in the adults.

'Academic self-image' refers to the pupil's own concept of how clever at schoolwork he or she is. To a disproportionate extent disruptive pupils feel themselves to be unable to do their school work.

In addition, sociometric data illuminated the disruptive pupils' relationships with other pupils. Pupils were asked to nominate those they would like to be with in class and those they would not like to be with, to yield information on popularity and unpopularity respectively. Popularity was not related to disruptiveness, disruptive pupils had neither a large nor particularly small number of friends. However, unpopularity was strongly related to disruptiveness: disruptive pupils were strongly disliked. This is consistent with the findings of Galloway *et al.*, (1982) who found that over one third of the sample of suspended pupils had few, if any, friends.

## 2.3  Explanations given by those involved

In giving explanations for their behaviour, disruptive pupils generally exonerate themselves. 'It was the teacher's fault' is the commonest explanation (Tattum, 1982), and Marsh *et al.*, (1978) found that disruptive pupils explained their behaviour as being retribution for teacher misdeeds such as nagging or unfairness.

Data on the backgrounds of the teachers who frequently suffer disruption have not been reported, but their attitudes to their pupils have been described (Hargreaves *et al.*, op.cit.). In essence such teachers put the blame for the disruption they suffered onto the pupils, just as the pupils put the blame on them. The result is impasse.

Our own work also investigated the descriptions teachers give of disruptive pupils. The constructs teachers most often used about disruptive pupils were 'malicious', 'rude', 'easily distracted', 'lazy', 'short attention span'. Disruptive pupils who scored low on social skills with adults were seen by teachers as malicious and rude, whereas those who scored low on academic self-image were more likely to be seen as easily distracted, lazy and having a short attention span. The implication is that the teachers were sensitive to the relevant characteristics of the pupils, but construed them in ways that removed the opportunity for intervention by the teacher.

## 2.4  The pupils and teachers involved in disruption

In summary it becomes possible to sketch a picture of pupils most likely to be involved in disruptive incidents. They are likely to be boys of below average ability, from disharmonious homes where their relationships with their parents are unsettled. At school they see themselves as being of low academic ability, and as getting on badly with staff. They are widely disliked by their peers, and are blamed by the teachers for the disruptive incidents they are involved in, while they themselves see the fault lying with the teachers and the school.

This is a sad picture and certainly not the happy carefree image of the best days of a person's life! The other side of the coin is not much brighter. The probable position of disrupted teachers can similarly be characterised. They know themselves to be failing in this pre-requisite skill of their profession. As a result their lessons are clearly not as intended, so they are failing professionally. They are evaluated as poor teachers by their pupils (and probably by their fellow teachers whether peers or superiors). They are blamed for disruptive incidents in their classes by the disruptive pupils, while in their turn they blame the pupils. It is small wonder that disruption leads to teacher stress.

From these two sketches, it appears that the two main protagonists in a disruptive incident are both suffering and suffering similarly.

Another important point comes from these findings. Trying to resolve this eventually damaging problem by using the explanations offered by the protagonists is unlikely to lead to progress. The views of those concerned directly and personally are too coloured by their need to protect their own self esteem so they tend to pin the blame on other people, or institutions, or circumstance.

**8**

In itself, this process of attributing success or failure to elements outside oneself is a worrying phenomenon. It has been widely demonstrated (for instance Kelly, H. and Michela, J., 1980) that such a tendency leads to people being unable to alter a situation. For instance, explaining an exam failure by reference to luck, the examiner or the weather rarely leads to subsequent success, whereas explaining it in terms of not having worked often does. The tendency for teachers and pupils to blame others for disruption helps a little to explain why the problem is hard to resolve.

As in resolving any problem of relationships, whether marital, industrial or international, the first task for the arbitrator is to establish some facts – facts about the events and behaviour that make up the relationship whether it is working positively or negatively.

For this reason it is essential for a teacher to know something about classroom behaviour in order to reduce classroom disruption. Once the behaviour is described, the more subjective aspects (the attitudes and explanations offered by those involved) can be interpreted in relation to the behaviour. The next chapter describes observations of classroom behaviour, and some of the results that have been obtained from such observations.

# Disruptive behaviour

## 3.1 Classroom observation

Teacher opens the door.

*Teacher* Come on in then!

Pupils come in, chatting.

*Teacher* Quietly now and sit down.
*Teacher* Craig, stop that.
*Teacher* Michael have you got your book today?
*Michael* No Miss.
*Teacher* I did remind you.
*Michael* I forgot Miss.
*Teacher* Right. Pay attention. Last time we drew rectangles in our books on
squared paper. Then we counted the number of squares, and that
way we found the area of each rectangle.
Open your books now and find the rectangles you drew.
*Michael* I haven't got a book Miss!
*Teacher* I'll give you some paper and you can start again Michael.
*Michael* Oh God.
*Teacher* I didn't hear that Michael.
Now – the rest of you – get out your rulers and measure the sides of
the rectangles. Write them next to the answers you got last time for
the area of each rectangle.
Here's some squared paper Michael. Start by drawing three
rectangles on it.
*Michael* What's the use of this Miss? It's boring.
*Teacher* When you get somewhere to live for yourself …
*Craig* Ya him and Susan.
*David* And their kid.

Laughter.

*Teacher* Now shut up and get on with your work.

This little scene could have occurred in most schools today. And here we
have the classroom behaviour of a disruptive pupil recorded on paper.
However for the purposes of analysing Michael's behaviour this recording has
its weaknesses.

First we have little indication of how much time Michael devoted to any single behaviour. Secondly we have no idea what he was doing while the teacher was talking, and thirdly we have no idea what any other pupil was doing. It could be that they were all chatting away and Michael alone was paying attention to the teacher during her speeches. These are all important things to know if we are to learn about the behaviour of pupils in class. Clearly, for purposes of analysis, play-script type recording does not suffice.

There is remarkably little work published that describes the behaviour of pupils in class so as to compare the behaviour of disruptive and non-disruptive pupils. The work of Flanders and those who have followed him have described teachers' talk in the classroom, and the corresponding talk of pupils (for instance Flanders, 1970). However that work tells us little about disruptive behaviour.

# 3.2  Findings of classroom observation

In the Oxford Study, the use (in a large number of lessons) of an observation schedule (an extended version of the schedule outlined in Chapter 6), has made it possible to describe the behaviour of disruptive pupils (Gray, 1987). These results can be summarised here, and they do offer some of the background information needed to understand disruptive pupils. It must be remembered in reading these findings that the work was done in a small town comprehensive not particularly noted for difficult pupils.

## a)  Amount of work done

The amount of work done by pupils in lessons varies widely. However it can often be depressingly low; figures of less than 10 per cent of the lesson were frequently being recorded and in every case these low figures were for identified disruptive pupils. The difference between identified disruptive and non-disruptive pupils in this respect was considerable. Average values for all the lessons observed showed that disruptive pupils worked for 50 per cent of lesson time, non-disruptive pupils for 70 per cent of the time.

## b)  Amount of misbehaviour

It comes as no surprise to know that disruptive pupils have been found to be engaged in misbehaviour more of the time than non-disruptive pupils. What is significant is that the identified disruptive pupils were misbehaving for roughly ten times as much of the time as the non-disruptive pupils. The averages were 9 per cent and 1 per cent respectively.

## c)  Activity switching

A less immediately obvious measure of pupil behaviour was suggested by interviews with teachers. Disruptive pupils were characterised as having short attention spans, or poor concentration, and these descriptions were borne out by the observation data. Disruptive pupils were found to switch their activities between consecutive observations roughly twice as often as the non-disruptive pupils.

## d)  Teachers as leaders, pupils as followers

By analysing both teacher and pupil data (factor analysis for the statistically minded) it was possible to see how the behaviour of pupils and teachers were related to each other.

It was possible to characterise the behaviour of those observed both in terms of how much work they were doing, and how socially pleasant they were being.

It became clear that pupils were most likely to work when the teacher was both concentrating on work, and being pleasant. Teachers being aggressive did not increase the amount of work done by pupils.

Equally important, it was found that the non-disruptive pupils were very much more responsive to the teacher's behaviour than were the disruptive pupils. In other words the disruptive pupils were not taking their cue from the teacher, they were largely ignoring him or her both in terms of working and in terms of their personal style. When the teacher was pleasant, the non-disruptive pupils were pleasant. When the teacher concentrated on work the non-disruptive pupils did the same. In both aspects, the disruptive pupils were comparatively uninfluenced by the teacher's behaviour.

All these findings support the teacher's point of view. Disruptive pupils *do* disrupt more than others, they *do* work less and they *do* have shorter attention spans, and they *are* generally more difficult to relate to.

However these conclusions, drawn from the observations of those pupils, are not the same as describing the pupils themselves as lazy or naughty. To use these two descriptions is to make assumptions as to the motives behind the pupil's behaviour, and such assumptions are unhelpful. From the direct observations it is possible to come to an understanding of pupil behaviour that could not be reached by using such descriptions of the *pupils* who are involved.

This last point will be considered further in Chapter 5, but first, in Chapter 4, it is necessary to consider some of the consequences of disruptive behaviour.

# Consequences of disruption

**4**

## 4.1 Immediate consequences

The immediate consequences of classroom disruption are all too familiar to anybody who has ever been in a classroom. Noise, anger, abuse, threats and violence all have to be considered as components of serious confrontations. Even if routine disruption does not escalate to this level, it is very clear that work, learning and teaching all become impossible in disrupted classrooms.

Furthermore the influence of a disruptive incident is out of all proportion to the numbers of individuals involved (McNamara, 1975). A serious confrontation between just one pupil and the teacher can stop the other thirty in the class working for some time. As we saw in the previous chapter, the teacher's style of interaction has an effect on the behaviour of non-disruptive pupils, so the residue of anger following a confrontation is bound to influence the class for the worse. The immediate consequence of disruption is the prevention of work and the damage done to the relationship between the teacher and all the members of the class (especially the disruptive pupils). However these are also longer-term effects.

## 4.2 Medium-term consequences

The medium-term consequence is liable to be the formal 'punishment' of the pupil. In many schools this is becoming a less regular direct response to disruption, but it is still worth considering it briefly. There is very little evidence that formal punishment prevents repetition of an offence. Formal punishment seems to do two things. It tends to increase the alienation of the punished, so if the pupil disliked the teacher before being punished, he will probably dislike him more afterwards (Redl and Wineman, 1951 and 1952). Secondly, punishment increases the pupil's identification with the negative or delinquent sub-culture of the school (Hargreaves, 1967).

Effective alternatives to punishment always sound rather limp, but many schools are shifting to incorporating responses to disruptive behaviour into the pastoral system. Similarly the provision in some schools of a 'time-out' facility (where pupils can go to 'cool down') offers a way of interrupting escalation, and hence of reducing the call for punishment. The use of contracts (formalised agreements between teacher and pupil about behaviour to be aimed for) does the same. Such methods have been used successfully in numerous special schools and units for disturbed children, as well as in mainstream schools (Topping, 1983). The reasons for this will be considered below in discussing the long-term consequences of disruption.

One other medium-term consequence also needs to be considered. The disruption reduces the amount of work that pupils do. The fact that disruptive pupils work less was established in the Oxford Study (see Chapter 3) and this is likely to reduce their acquisition of academic skills. In any school subject that is at all serial in nature (and most are), failure to learn one lesson must make the next more difficult. This fits with the findings (Rutter *et al.*, 1970) of a close link between reading failure and disruptive behaviour, and it is very likely that the one feeds the other, making it hard for the child to escape from either problem.

# 4.3 Long-term consequences

Two of the longer-term consequences have already been mentioned in discussing punishment above. They are increased alienation of pupils and identification with negative sub-groups. These can of course occur as a direct result of disruptive behaviour, and formal punishment is liable to emphasise them. Other long-term consequences can be considered under two headings – self-image and stress.

## a) Pupil self-image

The relationship between disruptive behaviour and lower achievement was mentioned above, but in the long-term there is an extra twist to the connection between the two. Repeated poor achievement must eventually lower the self-image of the pupil. If you fail in your work repeatedly, you come to think you are thick. In Chapter 2 this self-image was mentioned as one of the findings on the background attitudes of disruptive pupils studied. The suggestion is that this could be a result of disruptive behaviour. In the same chapter the teacher's perception of such problems was also mentioned; such pupils were seen as lazy.

In the same discussion the disruptive pupil's perception of their own social skills was also mentioned, and it was apparent that they saw themselves as unskilled at dealing with adults, and unable to influence such contracts. It is not hard to imagine that such views could be developed in a child whose regular contact with teachers is negative. Being told off frequently has to convey the message that you are not skilled at dealing with adults. Again the teachers' perception of this was in terms of 'rudeness'.

## b) Teacher self-image

It must not be imagined that it is only the pupils whose self-image is damaged by disruption. Teachers set great store by their capacity to control classes, and their professional self-esteem is undermined by failures to do so (see Cox, 1977). Pupils also place great emphasis on teachers' abilities to control a class, as was mentioned in Chapter 1. In fact Gannaway (1976) found that teachers who could not control a class were written off by pupils as useless.

In this context it must be borne in mind that some failure is inevitable in any profession or activity. Doctors do not cure every illness, accountants make mistakes and lawyers lose cases. Built into the ethos and structure of these professions are attitudes and supports for the individual in such circumstances. It seems to be a problem for teachers, more than for most other professionals, that their work is seen to involve the application of their own personality, undifferentiated from their professional role. The danger of this is that damage to their professional self-image also damages their personal self-image, so instead of feeling 'I am failing as a teacher' they feel 'I am failing as a person' which is even more damaging.

These long-term effects on the self-images of those involved in disruption are summed up in the table below.

| Observable effects of disruption | | Perception of individual concerned | Other person's perception |
|---|---|---|---|
| Pupil | Teacher | | |
| Poor achievement | | 'I'm thick.' | 'He's lazy.' |
| Negative contact with adults | | 'I can't deal with adults.' | 'He's rude.' |
| | Failure to teach lesson | 'I can't control kids.' | 'He's a useless teacher.' |

## c) Stress

The immediate effects of disruption mentioned at the beginning of this chapter included noise, anger, threats and violence and these produce stress and insecurity.

Stress in teachers has been identified as a major problem influencing the teacher in every aspect of life (Cox, op.cit.). However it is worth considering that confrontations are inevitably stressful for pupils also. So for both teacher and pupil there is immediate stress arising from disruption.

However for both there is also long-term stress, and this results from the conflict between their damaged self-images and the expectations of the situation. So the teacher who feels himself to be failing is daily confronted by the need to succeed, control a class and teach. The pupil who feels himself to be 'thick' is daily expected to do work which he feels unable to do. Despite his feeling of incapacity to relate to adults, the disruptive pupil has to do so regularly in class, and frequently he is expected to perform very difficult social moves like asking for help or apologising.

All these three conflicts generate stress and insecurity in the person concerned, and the effects of this are far reaching.

Two consequences of stress need to be considered at some length. The first, egocentricity, will be discussed here. It concerns the way that stress may colour a person's *understanding* of events. The second (which is the subject of Chapter 5) concerns the way that stress can directly affect a person's *actions*.

## d) An effect of stress – egocentricity

Try stopping a play-ground fight between Michael and Craig. A cleaned up version is likely to go rather like this:–

*Teacher* Michael, why did you hit him?
*Michael* He started it.
*Craig* No I didn't, he started it. He shoved me.
*Michael* No I didn't. He was trying to nick my bag.

*Craig*   No I wasn't, I was just trying to get my things back from him. He'd nicked by lunch and my books.

*Michael* ...

This can run and run, and most teachers would get fairly exasperated at the two boys forever blaming each other. The teacher in this case can well see that both boys are exonerating themselves, heaping the blame onto the other, and in no way seeing the other boy's point of view. In other words the two boys are being deeply egocentric.

This tendency of disruptive pupils to be egocentric has been found in the work of Tattum (1982) and Marsh *et al.* (1978). These investigations were mentioned in Chapter 2, and in both cases it was found that disruptive pupils put the blame on the teacher for their own disruptive behaviour.

However, a secure successful teacher knows that only when Michael and Craig have stopped fighting will it be possible to get some sense out of them. In that setting Michael may be able to see that Craig had a point, not that he just wanted a fight, but wanted to get his lunch back (even if that was a misunderstanding). In other words, in a calm setting it is possible to reduce the egocentricity of the two pupils. Egocentricity is a common response to stress; and it is an important one for teachers to understand.

Stress may be generated by being under threat. The treat may be real or imagined, physical or psychological, but the power of a threat depends on the damage it can inflict. In the case of psychological threats, the power depends on the individual being threatened. The more insecure a pupil, the more serious is the threat of an assault on his self-esteem. So if a pupil is really unconfident about his peer relationships, academic ability or his relationships with adults, threats to these things can be very serious. Then misunderstandings over a lunchbox or homework and being told off can all become major threats, to an already low self-esteem. The more insecure he is, the more serious the threat.

In the face of such a threat, one common defence is to be selective in seeing what is happening. So the threatened pupil can defend his inadequacy by only seeing the other person's faults. The more insecure he is, the more damaging would be an assault on his self-esteem, so the harder he must defend himself. As a defence this process of egocentric filtering works. Seeing the other person's faults leaves his own self-esteem intact. The underlying danger is that by being objective he might find out that he was wrong, and that would be catastrophic to an insecure individual. He can only afford to accept ideas that do not carry that threat. So defensive egocentricity works in the very short term. The stressful threat to self-esteem is avoided and the problem is understood in terms of the assumed motive of the other person. Unfortunately in the longer term this exacerbates the problem. Having laid the blame at the door of the other person, and having ascribed motives to him, the pupil perceives that he himself has no need to change (see Chapter 2).

This understanding of the apparently irrational egocentricity of disruptive pupils needs to be tempered with evidence that teachers can be in danger of doing the same. The 'Deviance – provocative' teacher of Hargreaves *et al.* (op.cit.) certainly appears to blame pupils for disruption (see Chapter 2). The teachers interviewed by Lawrence *et al.* (1984) appeared generally to do the same.

Disruptive behaviour is so defined because its consequences are disruptive. The mistake should not be made of thinking that these consequences of behaviour are also the goals of that behaviour. This mistake clearly is made by teachers when they describe pupils as malicious, rude, lazy etc., implying that this is what the pupils intend. This misattribution of motives to children with behaviour problems is common. The terms used really illustrate the effect on the describer rather than the true motivation of the child. In this way they can be seen as another example of egocentricity at work.

This egocentricity is highlighted by the fact that although teachers' ascriptions of rudeness or maliciousness reliably discriminated between disruptive and non-disruptive pupils, they failed to see which boys were unpopular with their peers (Howarth, 1985). This latter perception is of relationships not involving themselves whereas the former concerns relationships in which the teachers themselves are involved. In other words, these teachers tended to be egocentric in the sense that they accurately described the effects of the pupils' behaviour on themselves, but they were not good at describing relationships in which they themselves were not involved.

This warning that teachers can become egocentric must not be taken as teacher-bashing. It is a common human consequence of stress. Some teachers learn to make allowances for this reaction and go on to view pupils rather more dispassionately. Good teachers do not assume that pupils are getting at them, just as good pupils do not assume that teachers are picking on them.

## e) Reputations

The description of a 'good teacher' above was of a person who did not assume that pupils were deliberately disruptive. This lies at the heart of the description given by Hargreaves *et al.* (1975) of a 'good teacher' ('deviance-insulative' teacher in their terminology). Their work is important largely because it stresses one of the affects of stress induced egocentricity – the generation of reputations, or labels.

Reputations of pupils can so often be ossified versions of the teachers' egocentric view of them. So a pupil gains a reputation as disruptive when teachers follow a sequence of thought that goes like this.

1. Michael's behaviour disrupted my lesson.
2. Michael always disrupts my lessons.
3. Michael is disruptive (and ever shall be).

The first step, from 1 to 2, marks the move from an observation to a generalisation. In the second step, from 2 to 3, a description of *behaviour* becomes a description of the *person* – it becomes labelling – and so becomes a prediction. The change in tense from past to present, and on to future, gives the clue that this process has occurred.

The last of these steps emphasises the idea that disruption is a characteristic of Michael. Michael may frequently be involved in disruption but that is not to say that disruption is a characteristic of Michael. Disruption is perhaps characteristic of Michael's relationship with teachers, and it is useful to know more about a pupil who has such relationships, but that is not the same as saying he is disruptive. This danger of using the shorthand 'disruptive pupil' was discussed in Chapter 2, but the accurate description (a pupil whose interactions with teachers are characterised by disruptive behaviour) is too cumbersome to use.

The reputation of being disruptive divorces the pupil's behaviour from his relationship with the teacher. The reputation carries the implication that it is the pupil who has to change, and at the same time that the pupil is going to be very hard to change. A reputation is to 'give a dog a bad name', and that is proverbially hard for the pupil to escape from.

The effects of reputations operate on teachers just as they do on pupils. So teachers gain a reputation and this makes it harder for them to break out of a cycle of disruption. Reputations as 'unable to control a class' seriously exacerbate and perpetuate the problem. Put that way it is easy to see that a bad reputation can only increase the damage to a person's self-esteem or self-image, and some of the consequences of that will be discussed further in the next chapter.

# Understanding disruptive behaviour

## 5

In Chapter 4, one of the main consequences of disruption was identified as stress which often results in those involved becoming egocentric, thinking of the whole thing from their own point of view. One of the implications of this is that anybody wishing to *understand* disruption has to be somewhat cautious of using accounts of disruption given by those involved. Such accounts are important in that they reveal the point of view of the person involved, but to understand the behaviour requires a more detached stance.

It is worth noting in this context that nursery school and playgroup teachers in the Oxford Pre-school Project found that one of the most useful exercises they were involved in was simply sitting and watching pupils they would normally be busy coping with (Sylva *et al.*, 1980; Wood, 1980). Doing this can also give teachers the chance to watch the behaviour of pupils from a slightly detached point of view, and that is a most useful exercise (see Chapter 6).

Seen from a less involved perspective, the behaviour of disruptive pupils (see Chapter 3) becomes a little easier to understand. It is not a weird phenomenon unrelated to the rest of human behaviour. The behaviour of disruptive pupils can be understood, and many of the elements of it are extremely familiar to us in other contexts. Consideration of this is an important step in understanding disruptive behaviour.

Next time you have to go for a job interview try looking at your fellow applicants in the waiting-room. There they are tapping their feet, smoking, picking finger-nails, alternately gazing out of the window, and looking at a crossword, scratching and so on. When you get into the interview you have to beware of several things – blurting out answers to half asked questions, making exaggerated claims, and totally forgetting everything you know even to the extent of getting your address wrong.

All of these behaviours are the effect of stress/insecurity/frustration/fear (the words mean much the same thing), and there are others.

When you get home from work having been stuck in a traffic jam, a broken flower pot may receive a kick, the front door is likely to be well slammed, and animal welfare groups hope that you do not catch the cat on the kitchen table.

Most of these forms of behaviour are familiar to us in every-day life. Comparable behaviour occurs in class, but it is easy to overlook the parallels. The pupil who enters into a situation shouting 'easy-peasy' only to get it wrong is not unlike the interviewee who blurts out the wrong answers to simple questions. The pupil who picks a fight with the teacher after being questioned by the deputy-head about smoking is like the person who kicks the cat on getting home late.

Comparisons such as these may be interesting, but it is necessary to go a little further to appreciate fully that disruptive behaviour can be the direct effect of insecurity or stress. This can be tackled by considering three questions. First, what evidence is there that the behaviour of disruptive pupils is indeed a reflection of or effect of stress? Secondly, why is it that one individual responds to a situation by being disruptive when another does not? Thirdly, what evidence is there to support the idea that disruptive pupils are under stress – what could be causing their insecurity? These have to be considered one at a time, and it is always wisest to start from observations of behaviour.

# 5.1  Disruptive behaviour and insecurity

There are of course many forms of behaviour that disrupt lessons. There are also numerous behaviours that are characteristic of disruptive pupils. The danger of confusing the behaviour of these pupils, and the motives that they are sometimes assumed to have for their behaviour, was discussed in Chapter 4. So it is essential to avoid or at least analyse terms which assume a motive behind a pupil's behaviour. Once this is done, it is possible to see that most of the behaviour that disrupts lessons, and most of the behaviour that is characteristic of disruptive pupils has its roots in anxiety or insecurity.

This assertion may be questioned by teachers thinking of large swaggering domineering fifth form boys, but looking afresh at the actual behaviour of these pupils may make the point. There is such a range of behaviour that different aspects have to be considered one at a time. Many of the types of behaviour can be understood to an extent as an effect of the pupil's egocentricity. This was described in Chapter 4 as being a common consequence of stress or anxiety, but anxiety or insecurity also appears to underline many other forms of behaviour characteristic of disruptive pupils.

An additional problem is that behaviour can become fixed; part of a person's regular repertoire in rather the same way that nervous tics, gestures or turns of phrase can become established in the person's regular behaviour. So sometimes the origin of the behaviour can be obscure. However, by looking at situations where a particular form of behaviour occurs, it may be possible to understand it better, and understanding it has to be the starting point for reducing the problem.

## a)  Rudeness/flying off the handle

The discussion in Chapter 2 showed that one of the characteristics of disruptive pupils, from the teachers' point of view, was their tendency to be rude and malicious. Certainly it is understandable that the process of escalation may be seen in these terms.

The teacher asks the pupil to do something (to take a coat off, sit down or to pay attention) and gets a mouthful of abuse in return. This is one of the commonest and most worrying aspects of disruptive pupils' behaviour.

It is not enough to say that such behaviour is like the interviewee blurting out half-baked answers or that it is like the cat getting kicked. This behaviour can be understood in two ways and both are well researched aspects of anxiety behaviour.

The first of these is known as *over-intensity*. In a state of anxiety a person is likely to respond to half a cue, and to do so with unusual intensity. It has been established that over-intense behaviour is common where a person is unable to decide what to do. Phrases such as 'I suddenly saw red' are used to describe that moment, and generally it is seen as a moment of decision coming at the climax of mounting tension or anxiety. In these terms it is easy to see such outbursts towards the teacher as being based in anxiety.

Over-intensity also very well describes the behaviour of a child who shouts 'Don't you touch me' when the teacher tries to be nice to him. Such over-intense behaviour is often very confusing to the other party: it appears out of context and out of proportion to the situation. Seeing it as an effect of the child's anxiety can make it more intelligible.

The second form of anxiety behaviour that can be useful in understanding a pupil's escalating behaviour is known as *redirected behaviour*. The person who kicks the cat after a row at work is familiar enough. It may be his boss he is angry with, but since he can't afford to punch the boss, his anger is redirected to another object. It is essentially stressful situations that generate this sort of behaviour, and it is well established that people do respond to anxiety in this way. For pupils to respond to stress by redirecting anger towards the teacher may be unpleasant and worrying but viewed this way it is not totally foreign to them.

## b) Fighting/squabbling

Fighting between pupils is not in essence very different from a pupil confronting the teacher. The explanations for pupils getting into fights can be seen to be similar to those given above for challenges to the teacher although redirected behaviour is less likely to apply to pupil fights.

Anxious, insecure pupils are as likely to fly off the handle with their peers much as they are with their teachers. The secure pupil is able to tolerate teasing or provocation. He can avoid confrontation partly because his behaviour is not over-intense. The insecure pupil is liable to respond aggressively to a suspicion of a threat, whether physical or emotional, real or imagined.

## c) Shouting out/attention seeking

Pupils are often described by teachers as attention seeking. This is of course not a description. It is couched in terms of the teacher's assumptions of the pupil's motives for the behaviour. Behaviour such as shouting out, asking questions unrelated to work and not listening to the answers or making far more noise than anybody else when putting a bag on the desk may all be described as 'attention seeking'.

Attention seeking is a useful phrase as a starting point in understanding this behaviour. It is very normal for people to seek the attention of others; it is the normal way of starting a conversation. What these pupils do is they seek attention, gain attention but they do not follow up by having a conversation. In other words their behaviour is incomplete.

*Incomplete behaviour* is very much the partner of the over-intense behaviour described above. Having impulsively jumped into doing something, the insecure person suddenly finds himself doing something inappropriate and stressful, and stops doing it. The teacher's perception that the pupil is attention seeking is half right. He is seeking attention. The point is that the anxious pupil is unable to use the attention, his behaviour is impulsive and incomplete, which is disruptive and extremely frustrating for the teacher. It is also a classic form of anxiety-based behaviour.

## d) Being unsettled

One of the characteristics of disruptive pupils described in Chapter 2 was the fact that they were found to switch activities more frequently than other pupils. This was described by teachers as being easily distracted, or having poor concentration.

This can be viewed as being similar to the behaviour described as attention seeking. Having started doing one thing, the anxious pupil is likely to respond suddenly to a cue that sets him off doing something else. Being insecure, the child has a low frustration tolerance; the slightest difficulty or even a short pause between two parts of an activity, leads the child to switch attention away from that activity. Thus he gives up easily, does not stick with a task and is easily distracted. It is a common observation that a child's distractability varies from class to class and subject to subject. It varies according to the difficulty of the subject, the motivation to do it, the distractions in the environment and the child's general feeling of security or insecurity at the time.

## e) Fidgeting

Fidgeting, playing with things or fiddling with materials are characteristics of many disruptive pupils. Behaviours like these are often seen as responses to anxiety, as are scratching, grooming, doodling and arranging (and re-arranging) books, pens, rulers etc.

Behaviour like this is referred to by ethologists (e.g. Tinbergen, 1952) as *displacement activity* and is generally seen as an indication that a person is frustrated or torn between doing two or more things, so does a third (irrelevant) thing instead. As a 'solution' to stress, fidgeting involves carrying out a safe, well rehearsed set of actions. At a time when a person is failing to do the main activities of the moment, at least he is succeeding in doodling, scratching his head, fiddling with a pencil or whatever. It is a way of calming ourselves, for success relaxes whereas failure provokes anxiety. Many of the same activities – especially scratching, stretching etc – can be seen as people calm themselves and prepare to go to sleep.

## f) Making odd noises/babyish behaviour

Quite frequently disruptive pupils are described as shouting out odd phrases, words or noises in class. To an extent these can be understood in much the same way as the behaviour described as 'attention seeking' discussed above. However in some instances these odd noises have an added element.

The noises are often baby-like, ritualised and repeated like small children making noises. Comparable behaviour is also found when pupils talk in a baby voice. This *regressive behaviour* is again a response to stress, and consists of using behaviour characteristics of the person when younger.

## g) Conclusion

Disruptive behaviour arises then out of insecurity/stress and is characterised by impulsiveness, carelessness, incompleteness (activities easily given up), fast activity switching, regression, aggression and/or irrelevance. Any one incident can have more than one characteristic. They are all typical of individuals when stressed/insecure, when frustrated or in motivational conflict (see Hinde, 1970; Argyle, 1978 and footnote*).

This still leaves two of our questions unanswered. Why do some individuals exhibit these behaviours when others do not and what is generating the stress for these pupils.

## 5.2 Individual variations

It is important to consider the question of why one individual exhibits stress-based behaviour, and another does not.

Individual differences exist at birth, and the 10 per cent or so of babies who are 'difficult' – miserable, difficult to comfort, react badly to new situations, have irregular rhythms of sleep or feeding, change levels of alertness suddenly – are much more likely (but are not inevitably predestined) to become difficult toddlers, pre-schoolers and school age children (e.g. Thomas *et al.*, 1968). The behaviour shown is very similar to the stress-driven behaviour we have just described in Section 5.1.

In addition to temperamental differences at birth, life experiences of the sort described in Section 2.2 predispose children to behaviour problems, and to being disruptive in class.

The contribution of the various factors differs from individual to individual, but the final outcome, the final common development path, is a pupil who, in class, is insecure/easily frustrated/easily stressed/lacking in confidence/anxious etc. (the words refer to much the same thing). In the classroom, the resulting behaviour is often disruptive.

## 5.3 Sources of classroom stress

There is a source of stress which is very general, but is often overlooked. This is the conflict between a person's self-image and the expectations made of him or her. Exams, interviews or performing on stage are prime examples of this, but any situation in which a person feels that the expectations are too high can do the same.

In Chapter 2 the self-images of disruptive pupils were discussed, and they were found to have unusually poor self-images. Confronted with normal expectations they are likely to fear failure which is a recipe for insecurity. In the classroom this operates in two major areas, and in both cases disruptive pupils find themselves locked into vicious circles.

In relation to classroom tasks, insecurity leads pupils to switch attention more often, to work less therefore, to be over-intense or to perform displacement activities. This is seen as day dreaming, carelessness, distractability and some of these activities are seen as disruptive. This in turn leads to performance and learning being poorer. This link is made stronger if the lessons are inappropriately presented or if the child has a low IQ or a specific learning difficulty. Since the child performs less well there are fewer rewards both from the teacher and intrinsically from the work. This is

---

*The behaviours described will be familiar to ethologists as 'motivational conflict behaviours' i.e. behaviour shown when two or more motivations are simultaneously activated. The resulting behaviour can take many different forms. The forms described here are the result of conflict between fear motivation and some other motivation(s). Fear and frustration have similar physiological and behavioural effects. By definition insecure individuals are fearful, or are easily made so. Terms such as 'stressed' or 'anxious' are here from a behavioural point of view, best viewed as synonyms for 'fear/frustration/insecurity'.

exacerbated if the teacher's style is not terribly rewarding. This reduces the child's confidence and exacerbates his insecurity. Insecurity derived from other sources such as home, may spill over and promote this link, but it can be seen that the whole situation is liable to get progressively worse.

Looking at social relationships, insecurity again leads to attention switching, over-intensity, regressive behaviour, redirected behaviour, redirected aggression. This leads to interactions being unsuccessful and therefore fewer social skills being learnt. The unsuccessful interactions mean that a hostile, non-co-operative relationship is negotiated with the teacher and often with other pupils. This in turn reduces the child's confidence and so on round in a vicious circle (see Figure 5.1). He may not be helped by having poor models and inconsistent disipline at home. His anxiety may also be directly affected by neurological factors and more recently it has been found, by dietary and related factors.

This 'process' view of disruptive behaviour and the factors which maintain it implies that the causes of one pupil's disruption may be different from the causes of another pupil's disruption. Similarly it implies that the vicious circles may be broken at points which are different from the entry of major causal factors. In other words good teaching can compensate.

It is important to compare Figure 5.1 with Figure 5.2. In 5.2, a comparable vicious circle is drawn up for the effects of disruption on a teacher. There the important effect of classroom disruption is the lowered professional (and arguably personal) self-image of the teacher. The conflict between this and the expectations of the teacher were discussed in Chapter 4, as was the possible outcome of increased egocentricity. If this leads the teacher to blame the pupils and to ascribe to them the motive of wanting to disrupt lessons, it is less likely that he or she will adjust his teaching to their needs. Less appropriate teaching is highly likely to lead to increased disruption and the vicious circle is complete.

From these understandings of disruption, it appears that pupils and teachers are interlocked in circles of damaging and self-damaging behaviour. The management strategies suggested in the rest of this book offer ways of breaking these vicious circles and keeping them broken, so reducing disruption and aiding learning. There are of course limits to what the individual classroom teacher can do, but in many classrooms those limits have not been reached.

**Figure 5.1**

Pupils' vicious circles

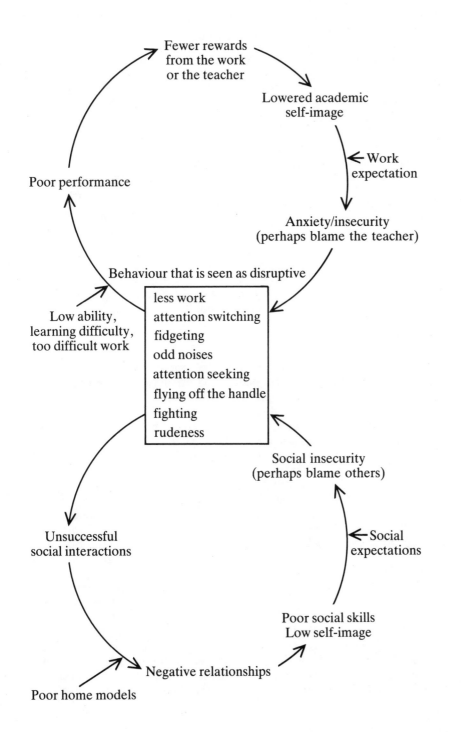

**Figure 5.2**

Teachers' vicious circle

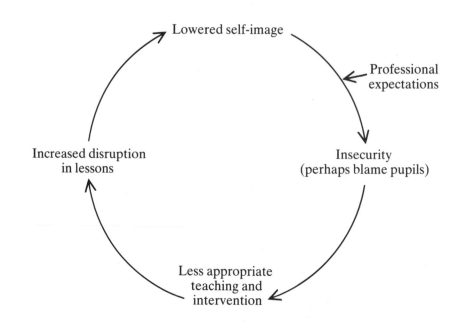

Before moving on to consider such strategies, one more question has to be discussed. Why is it that such emphasis is placed on two aspects of pupil behaviour, their work and their social performance?

The reason for this is twofold. First, as was mentioned in Chapter 2, these were the two elements that were found to distinguish disruptive pupils from others; the disruptive pupils had low self-image in these two areas. This is part of the justification for advancing the two circles in Figure 5.1.

The second reason is that these are the two predominant dimensions that make up the agenda for classrooms. In fact, these two dimensions have generally been found to be the most significant areas in terms of the skill of being a leader. Effective leaders have been shown (see for instance Hollander, 1975) to meet the needs or wants of their followers in these two respects. So, effective leaders help their followers to achieve the tasks of the group, and in addition they must afford personal social recognition to their followers, treat them decently as human beings.

It must be expected that frustration on either of these two dimensions would lead to conflict between leader and followers, teacher and pupils.

Almost all the advice offered to teachers even including that based on the idea of behaviour modification (Yule *et al.*, 1984) can be construed in terms of facilitating these processes, encouraging the work or relating to pupils in personal terms. In so doing the teacher is meeting his pupils' expectations of him, and thereby helping them to resolve their anxieties in more socially acceptable and functional ways. This lies at the heart of effective teaching.

# Investigating classroom disruption

## 6

The preceding chapters have been based on research and theory in the literature. Additional material has come from the author's own research, published in detail elsewhere (Gray, *et al.,* 1986; Gray, 1987). This makes it possible for our ideas to be evaluated, tested, confirmed or refuted. In addition our hope is that a large portion of our readership should be teachers, whether in post or in training, and teachers are in a position to check what we have written from direct and immediate observation in schools.

This chapter is intended to help teachers, *and especially student teachers,* to see whether the previous chapters make sense. The activities outlined can be used in a series of additional ways. They could be used as suggestions of methodology for action research in school or for the extended projects that many student teachers undertake. Perhaps the very best use would be as the basis for a course on classroom control, whether this is part of initial training, in-service training or a school-based initiative.

A series of activities – ways of finding out about disruption – are suggested. In each case findings predicted from other research are indicated, for comparison, although the references have been omitted when they accompany the full discussions of these points in preceding chapters.

## 6.1  What do pupils do in class?

The basis for understanding disruptive behaviour is an understanding of pupil behaviour generally.

However it is not very helpful to either look for or base your actions on supposed personality labels. Labels such as 'lazy', 'immature', 'poor home', 'stupid' or 'deliberately trying to provoke me' can colour your perception of a child.

For student teachers, lesson observation is a normal part of their school-based work. Teachers in post may have to take the initiative of arranging such opportunities. Doing so without worrying the other teacher can be a problem. The most persuasive argument is often along the lines of wanting to learn more about a particular pupil; knowing how he responds to a range of situations may be to the benefit of all the staff. Obviously such a session has to be followed-up with a discussion with the teacher who was observed in action. Reciprocal arrangements, when colleagues arrange to observe pupils in one another's classes, can be helpful.

Classroom observation
● In order to be really useful, classroom observation has to be structured.
● Spend some time while observing lessons watching 2–3 pupils only. Note the proportion of time spent working, chatting and messing about. Note their reactions to frustration. Note their application to the tasks set and their concentration spans. Get a feel for the flow of behaviour – after a while you may find yourself predicting what the pupil is about to do.

We have found that contrary to superficial appearances, the disruptive child in class and usually elsewhere, lacks confidence and self-esteem. He finds it difficult to concentrate, he is often impulsive and careless. He gives up easily on his work.

The short concentration span of many disruptive pupils usually shows itself in frequent switching from one activity to another. This can be very irritating to a teacher since these children never seem to be working, and never seem to settle. However it is all too easy to blame these children rather than to compensate for their need for support and clarity.

The rather loose lesson-observation suggested above will give an indication of the pupils' behaviour. However, for anybody wishing to do a more detailed study of the behaviour of pupils or the relationship between pupil behaviour and teacher behaviour, the following schedule is offered in Figure 6.1. It is often quite demanding to use but produces powerful results.

**Figure 6.1**

Detailed classroom observation

**Pupil observations**

| *Categories* | The child is: |
| --- | --- |
| **Work**ing | Predominantly engaged in the work set. |
| **Work related** | Involved in activities peripheral to work – e.g. hand up, waiting for teacher, getting materials. |
| **Fidg**et | Day dreaming, doodling etc. – solitary behaviour. |
| **Chat**ting | Talking (other than about work) to neighbouring children. |
| **Mild Dis**ruption | Engaged in solitary misbehaviour, misuse of equipment, illicit movement etc. |
| **Dis**ruption | Shouting to pupils, attacking/unsettling pupils, challenging teacher etc. |

**Teacher observations**

| *Categories* | The teacher is: |
| --- | --- |
| **Aggr**essive/Dominates | Restraining/holding pupils, shouting, insulting, abusing, threatening. |
| **Contr**olling | Commanding, nagging. |
| **Work**ing | Talking to the class or to part of it about work, discussing work with pupils. |
| **Accepting** | Chatting with pupils, praising pupils. |
| **Soci**able | Smiling, sharing a joke. |

It is possible to observe two pupils and the teacher in one lesson using the schedule shown in Figure 6.1. If one pupil is a known disrupter, and the other not, this will make comparison possible. Observations should be made of the three individuals in strict rotation, at precise time intervals – every 5 seconds is possible but every 10 seconds is easier. In this case the behaviour of each of the three (teacher, disruptive and non-disruptive) is recorded every 30 seconds. This is done by writing down the four letter code for the category (e.g. WREL for 'work related behaviour'). It is important to note that what is recorded is the behaviour of the individual at the time of recording (i.e. on the tenth second or whatever) not an overall impression of what has happened over the preceding 30 seconds.

The product of observations on this schedule look like this:

| 0 Teacher | 10 Target | 20 Control | 30 Teacher | 40 Target | 50 Control |
|-----------|-----------|------------|------------|-----------|------------|
| SOCL | MDIS | CHAT | SOCL | MDIS | CHAT |
| CONT | MDIS | WREL | CONT | FIDG | WREL |
| WORK | CHAT | WORK | WORK | MDIS | WORK |
| WORK | WREL | WORK | WORK | CHAT | WORK |
| ACPT | WREL | WORK | WORK | MDIS | WORK |

In Chapter 3 some indications are given of how to analyse such data, and of some of the results that have been obtained.

# 6.2  What forms does disruption take?

From the teacher's point of view, there are numerous forms of misbehaviour in class. However these are not all equally disruptive. Misbehaviour of these different types becomes disruptive if it significantly comes to interrupt the lesson. In this way there are several forms of disruption.

**Types of disruption**
In observing lessons, note what form any disruptive incident takes. The following is offered as a series of types of disruption.

1. Social interactions with peers. This covers chatting, horse play, note passing etc.
2. Conflict between pupils, fighting etc.
3. Planned group jokes. These are practical jokes usually at the teacher's expense.
4. Out of context trouble. This is the case of the pupil whose misbehaviour results directly to events outside the classroom e.g. arriving in class swearing about another teacher.
5. Personal conflict. This is the direct confrontation between a pupil and the teacher.
6. Individual bizarre behaviour – odd noises etc.

These categories of disruption are obviously slightly blurred at the edges, but useful for all that.

It is common for one form of trouble to develop into another, for instance for chatting (Type 1) to change into direct confrontation (Type 5) if the teacher's intervention is inappropriate.

Clearly these different forms of misbehaviour are described here in terms of the observer's inference as to what lay behind the behaviour. For this reason it is very different from the detailed observation schedules offered above in Section 6.1. It is useful to relate these types of disruption to the understandings of the phenomenon offered in Chapter 5.

## 6.3  How do pupils relate to adults?

Relating to authority figures requires a set of skills, which schools and teachers expect pupils to have.

Watch a child being told off and note the deferential moves that the teacher requires him or her to make.

We have found that disruptive children characteristically have very low ability to deal with adults and this is even more the case with authority figures such as teachers. When a really successful teacher has to tell a child off, notice that he or she will avoid demanding complete self-abasement; there is a danger of simply producing future resentment. It is also much harder for the child to accept the authority of an adult in front of his peers. The more inadequate the child the harder it is for him to back down.

## 6.4  How do disruptive pupils relate to their peers?

Observe some of the children in the play ground during break. Look out particularly for the ones that were disruptive in the lesson. Note what types of interaction they are involved in. Note whether they are involved in fights (real or mock). Note whether they are co-operating with other children or whether they are isolated, or rebuffed.

There is a popular myth among teachers, based perhaps on the Billy Bunter stories, that disruptive pupils are popular stars of the classroom. Analysis with sociograms shows that this is simply not true. Disruptive pupils are unpopular. They have a number of friends, but outside that small clique, they are widely disliked.

## 6.5  What difficulties do disruptive pupils bring with them to school?

In Chapter 2 several areas of the background of disruptive pupils were discussed as being relevant to their behaviour.

- Ask members of staff, particularly tutors, about the backgrounds of pupils who have come to your attention, either by observation or reputation.
- If appropriate and permitted in school, look at a *pupil's file* to find out more about his or her background.

Among disruptive pupils there is a high probability of finding unhappy homes, parents who don't get on or are separated. Many of these children are harshly treated or neglected. Tragically there is little that teachers can do about these factors, although a positive attitude from the school generally can help considerably in the long term (cf Rutter *et al.*, 1979). However there are other factors, associated with disruptive behaviour, that a classroom teacher can do something to compensate for. These include:

- low ability;
- specific learning difficulties;
- physical disabilities ranging from clumsiness/incoordination through partial hearing loss or speech problems to epilepsy.

Disruptive children rarely have all of these difficulties. Many have none of them. But they do come up more frequently among the children who disrupt lessons, so it can be helpful to look out for such problems to help your understanding of disruptive children. Although as labels they are of little use, such observations are important in suggesting a course of action by the teacher.

An additional point is that some relevant problems can vary from day to day. This can be illustrated from your own experience.

For one week make a daily note of your own attitude to work on a ten point scale. Note also the factors that make for good and bad days. How many of these applied when you were a child? What comparable factors did apply?

Pupils are like the rest of us, their moods vary, so it is important to consider the way the child is performing today. On some days disruption will be greater than on others. Occasionally it is possible to see why, more commonly not. It may be that home is disturbed that day, or that he has just come from a disliked lesson. As a teacher you can only be aware of these possibilities, and not base your expectations of either success or disaster on single lessons.

# 6.6 What are pupils' perceptions of school?

Most pupils will grumble about having to go to school. Most adults in a pub grumble about work, so school pupils are definitely not abnormal in this. However specific complaints can be informative.

In discussions with pupils find out:
- which activities they like best;
- which activities they like least;
- which activities they describe as 'work';
- which activities they describe as 'fun';
- which activities they describe as 'interesting';
- which activities they describe as 'boring'.

Outings are generally noted as the best thing school offers. Writing is most commonly described as 'work' (Gannaway, 1976).

The exact results on this type of opinion poll vary, but the number of 'don't knows' is generally small. Pupils have strong feelings about school, which is hardly surprising since it is a major part of their lives.

## 6.7  What do pupils think of your lessons?

It is perfectly feasible to get direct feedback from your pupils about your own lessons. Given a little time to discuss it, pupils will generally let you know their reactions to both content and lesson style.

For more structured feedback, ask pupils to keep a diary, attached to the work they do for you, giving a few lines on each lesson.

Asking pupils for their comments not only gives you information, it also helps them feel more involved in the work.

## 6.8  How do pupils judge teachers?

With diplomacy it is possible, and instructive to discover the criteria pupils use to judge teachers. These individual judgements should not be taken as 'fact' but do give an idea of the pupils' point of view.

In discussion with pupils, the names of staff members often crop up, generally with an evaluation attached 'She's O.K.', 'He's lousy' etc. The follow-up question 'Why, in what way is he lousy?' will often reveal the criterion of assessment.

In judging their teachers the first criterion has been found to be the ability to control the class: failure at this hurdle is damning. Pupils also like teachers who show some interest in the pupils they teach and some enthusiasm for the subject they are teaching. Pupils expect to be taught something in school. They like a sense of order and of fair play. They do not like teachers who pick on a child, however bad the child might be. They do not like teachers who try to step right out of role to be gang members with the kids.

# 6.9 How do teachers judge pupils?

End of term reports generally concentrate on two forms of judgement of pupils, academic achievemnt and effort. There may also be passing reference to other aspects of a pupil that staff think significant.

However there are also several other ways in which staff differentiate between pupils. These become apparent either in discussions with teachers about pupils, or just from overheard descriptions in the staff room. The terminology used is often flowery, but suggests what concepts are underpinning the description.

- In discussions with teachers be aware of the descriptions of pupils that are used. Work out what underlying concepts these descriptions relate to. Work out a hierarchy of judgements that are applied. For instance 'I will say this for him, he is not X, but he is very Y'. The implication is that the pupil passed the test of X but subsequently failed on test Y, so X was the first criterion used.
- It is important, especially for student teachers, not to become a spy in the staffroom, merely to be analytic about discussions.

Seven main areas of construct have been identified by Hargreaves *et al.* (1975). They found that all these were used early in the process whereby teachers reached a stable description of a pupil. The seven (with examples in brackets) were:

- appearance (short, fat, untidy);
- conformity to expectations in discipline (noisy, truculent);
- conformity to expectations in academic areas (bright, thick, lazy);
- likeability (pleasant girl, nice lad);
- peer group relations (leader, bully);
- personality (aggressive, easy-going);
- deviant (nuisance, pert, naughty).

Two points are worth noting on these categories.

**1.** There seems to be considerable overlap in these but they give an indication of how pupils are judged.

**2.** According to these authors, with time and extended contact with a pupil, teachers increase the emphasis placed on the categories that are inferential. Most important of these is 'motive elaboration', in other words ascribing to the disruptive pupil the motive of wishing to disrupt. This form of egocentricity has been discussed in Chapters 4 and 5.

# 6.10 What are the differences between successful and unsuccessful lessons?

It is a truism that lessons vary, but trying to identify the differences is not easy.

**Lesson observation**
If you can observe lessons, look out particularly for the following:

- How generally successful was the lesson?
- How well was the lesson prepared?
- Was the teacher's general style loud or quiet, aggressive or pleasant?
- Did the teacher move about the classroom or remain behind the desk?
- Was the teacher talking to pupils about things other than work?
- How much work was covered?
- What proportion of time was spent working as against socialising?
- How much scope was there for original rather than routine work?

Look through exercise books; note the quality, quantity and presentation of work done.

Note the incidents of disruption and how they were dealt with.

Video your own lessons. Most schools now have video camera and recorders, and they are straightforward to use. It does not require an operator on the camera to get a very usable recording of a lesson. Set up the camera with a wide-angle lens at the side of the classroom and let it run.

The recording can be for your eyes only, but can help enormously. Look out particularly for the ideas described under 'Lesson observation' above. In addition look out for other aspects of your own performance:

- Did you miss early signs of trouble?
- Did you effectively deal with trouble?
- Did you help to reduce anxieties about work?
- Did you make adequate personal recognition of individual pupils?
- Did you appear to be pleasant, relaxed and in control?
- How did pupils respond to you?

These are impossible to assess while teaching a lesson, but can be considered while watching yourself on play-back.

## 6.11 Summary

The items that make up this chapter have been thought out so as to help teachers view the phenomenon of disruption as dispassionately and constructively as possible. The idea has been to help teachers obtain an objective perception of disruption.

To progress from these perspectives it is vital to have an overall understanding of the phenomenon, and Chapters 4 and 5 offered such a synthesis. But the next step is towards doing something about the problem, and Part 2 takes that step.

# Part 2  What to do

# Introduction

In Chapter 2, numerous elements were identified from the literature as being related to disruptive behaviour in the classroom. The ideas developed in the remainder of Part 1 attempted to incorporate most of these into a coherent picture (see Chapter 5). Several of these elements are outside the sphere of influence of the teacher, especially the student or the junior teacher. But it was emphasised in Chapter 5 that change could be brought about, the vicious circle of disruption broken, by intervention at points other than the origin of a pupil's problems. One of these is very much in the sphere of influence of the teacher: it is his or her own classroom interaction with the pupil.

It is a commonplace observation that some teachers suffer more disruption than others (see Chapter 2). This is not magic, it is not personal chemistry, it is not that good teachers are born rather than made. There are analysable skills to the job of teaching which reduce disruption, and to do so is a necessary pre-requisite for learning to occur. This therefore poses the question 'What can I do to reduce disruption in my class?'.

The answer to this comes in four parts.

First it is important to have an understanding of the problem, its causes and the factors that perpetrate disruption. The first part of this book offers such an explanation. Without this basic appreciation, any recommendations would be rootless, subjective and liable to be misunderstood or forgotten, like any other arbitrary list.

Secondly, good teachers do their homework. Time spent preparing lessons is not time wasted, but certain elements of preparation are all too easily overlooked. Anti-disruption aspects of lesson-preparation are described in Chapter 7, based on the ideas developed in Part 1 of the book.

Thirdly, the behaviour of teachers in class varies considerably. It would be extraordinary if these variations did not influence the behaviour of the pupils, and a fair proportion of our work and the work of others has assessed that influence. This work on the general classroom behaviour of teachers, and its effects underlies Chapter 8 and its series of recommendations.

Fourthly, a certain amount of misbehaviour in class is inevitable. However, for this to have a real disruptive effect depends on whether it spreads to other pupils and escalates or is defused, contained and decreased. The task of reducing the disruptive effects of such misbehaviour is very much part of the teacher's role, and the way in which the teacher intervenes has a considerable influence on the outcome. Recommendations for this skill make up Chapter 9.

It must be stressed again that the suggestions in the following chapters are based on the ideas developed in the preceding section. The suggestions given are not new and cannot pretend to be comprehensive. Teaching of one form or another has to be one of the oldest professions so most sensible ideas have been tried already. The intention is to systematise good ideas, base them in a sound theory, and use them to exemplify the application of that theory.

# Anticipation

**7**

As a teacher, your capacity to reduce classroom disruption starts long before you go into the classroom. There are several jobs you can do in anticipation of meeting a class. Some involve finding out about the situation, others come under the general heading of 'lesson planning'.

This division of pre-lesson tasks into finding out and planning is of course a false one. It really is unrealistic to plan a lesson without having the relevant background information available. It would be like planning a journey without knowing whether you will travel by plane or by pony to Stockholm or Sydney.

## 7.1 Gathering information

As a basis for your teaching, you need information at all kinds of levels.

The suggestions set out might appear excessive in practice. The intention is to offer as full a list as possible. In practice time or opportunities will reduce the scope for action, but useful information could be gathered from all these areas.

### a) The school ✓

Knowing about the school serves several important purposes.

**1.** Knowledge about the structure and running of the school will give you confidence in your dealings with pupils. You need to know the rules if you are to feel confident in applying them.

**2.** You can gain a great deal of credibility by using the appropriate terminology and accepted systems.

**3.** You will have a far greater support from other staff if your early efforts have been within the bounds of normal accepted behaviour for the school.

These points are not intended to dampen originality, but teachers have to remember that they operate within an established system, and have to start from the status quo. The classroom is certainly the place to improve your teaching skills, but it is not a good place from which to alter the school structure.

*General school practice*

Ask about the school structure, e.g. setting, streaming, tutor group system, house system, rewards and punishments, exam syllabuses.

Look around the school and get a feeling for what the pupils expect to experience in class. In particular find out:

- how classes are taught generally, (whole class, group, individual);
- what materials are used (textbooks, handouts, individual topics);
- what teaching aids are used (OHP, video, cassettes);
- what levels of noise are normal;
- what levels of movement are normal;
- what degree of autonomy the pupils are given;
- whether first names or surnames are used when staff address pupils.

Many schools have clear and stated policies on subjects such as these, and it is wise to stick to them. Such whole school policies and systems can be invaluable to the individual teacher, and should be encouraged.

*Back-up*

Classroom disruption can be a threatening, alarming and lonely prospect for a teacher. Just the knowledge that support can be called on makes it less threatening, and this itself makes you more able to handle a problem.

Support may be available at different levels in the school hierarchy. It may also be either formal or informal.

- Find out what support is available officially.
- Find out what forms of support other teachers use.
- Find out which forms of support are the most successful.

Don't be afraid to ask direct questions about back-up. If you do need to call on help, knowledge in advance of what to do will be invaluable. If you don't, the knowledge will be support in itself, and will show others that you are serious about the job.

## b) The class

Any teacher will confirm that classes vary considerably. As a teacher you have to relate to the entire class, and have to do so in terms of the two dimensions of group performance 'task' and 'social' (see Chapter 5).

Information about the class can be gained from:–

**1.** Observation, where possible. It is valuable to observe classes that you are going to teach with their present teacher. Ideas for observation and things to look for are listed on the next page.

**2.** Other teachers' comments. These are always useful, but remember that you will be getting a personal perspective that may reflect the individual's relationship with the class.

## Work aspects

Information about the work that a class has been doing is generally available from the previous teacher or head of department. However it is useful to go beyond that.

Ask the previous teacher:

- how quickly topics were covered;
- which bits of work were popular or unpopular;
- which materials or methods were successful or unsuccessful.

If possible ask the pupils what they think of the different topics.

## Social aspects

To avoid simply accepting somebody else's prejudices the following points are helpful:

- Try to get descriptions of specific incidents or facts rather than global interpretations and impressions.
- Talk to more than one member of staff about the class.
- Find out what sub-groups form themselves in the class, and which require most attention or direction.
- Ask how the class is split up for group work.
- Ask how the class is divided for other subjects.

These will give you some idea of the social group that you are going to be working with. That grouping is important, but do not forget that teachers' perceptions of pupil groupings and peer relationships are not always reliable. In particular their estimates of the popularity of disruptive pupils tends to be on the high side (see Chapter 4).

## c) Individual pupils

In your discussions with teachers, individual names will undoubtedly crop up. You can get more information on individuals from several sources.

Once again discussions with a wide range of teachers can reduce the effect of one individual's perceptions being all that you learn. But still beware, pupils develop reputations that can be out of all proportion to their actual behaviour.

Try to find out about pupils in terms of both their work and their social functioning: they are both important in relation to classroom behaviours.

42

Find out about individuals from the following:

**1.** Your own classroom observations.
**2. Reports.** Use the school files to find out more about an individual pupil. Look for:
- sports achievements;
- outside interests;
- club membership;
- details of particular incidents;
- medical problems;
- home background;
- details of punishments.

**3. Special Needs.** It is important to know if pupils with other identified special needs e.g.
- specific learning difficulties e.g. backwardness at reading;
- perceptual – motor problems e.g. poor handwriting;
- poor memory;
- hearing problems;
- visual problems;
- speech problems;
- general low abilities;
- chronic medical conditions e.g. epilepsy.

**Remember:** Disruptive pupils often have learning difficulties.

These problems and appropriate methods of helping pupils overcome their affects are discussed in other volumes in this series.

**4. Test results.** The school may have such records of text results on a pupil, for instance:
- literacy;
- numeracy;
- verbal reasoning quotient.

**5. Staff comments.** Members of staff are often prepared to comment on pupils (see also Chapter 6). In interpreting these comments it is essential to avoid accepting the subjective (egocentric) aspects of them (see Chapters 4 and 5). You need an *objective* assessment of the pupil on which to base your interactions with him. The following two rephrasings were supported by our findings (Gray *et al.*, 1987).

'lazy'

A pupil described as      or      has a low academic self-image.

'distractible'

'rude'

A pupil described as      or      has little confidence or skill at relating to adults.

'malicious'

In the following chapters, the full significance of these two objective descriptions will be discussed.

## d) Your own teaching

Some of the most important information to use in lesson planning comes from your own previous lessons. The success or otherwise of your previous contact with a particular class reflects many of the other elements discussed in this section. However, assessment of your own lesson has to be carried out objectively, and your mark-book is a good vehicle for this.

Use your mark book. Keep your mark book up to date. It will help you to assess lessons that you teach, and enable you to see the levels of understanding, effort, enjoyment and work of the individual pupils.

Such records obviously focus on the work element of the lesson, and are important for that. In addition it is worth noting particular topics or methods that were positively or negatively received.

Keeping note of the social functioning of the group is less easy than recording the achievement of work. However noting successful and disruptive groupings can be useful for future reference.

At another level it is useful to keep a note of how you are getting on over time, this enables you to look back with clarity at what actually happened as opposed to the somewhat coloured view that you might have otherwise.

Keep a dispassionate record of lessons you teach along the following lines:
• How many of the pupils were well behaved?
• How much work did the class generally get done?
• If trouble did develop, did it spread, or did you manage to contain it?
• Did you manage to resolve the problems that developed?
• What would you like to have done differently?
• If problems did not arise, why not?

Records like this combine the work and social assessments of lessons and make it possible to review progress generally.

Reviews of lessons afterwards are of enormous benefit in evaluating whole lessons retrospectively, and in planning future lessons. However the process of reflective teaching should be part of the lesson as it progresses.

• Monitor the progress of the lesson as it goes along.
• Build in opportunities for review throughout the lesson plan. The occasional 30 second pause for reflection can enable you to do this dispassionately.
• Evaluate the progress of the lesson, and assess each phase of a lesson before you embark on a transition to a new phase. This evaluation may determine the way in which you make the transition, the timing of it or even the desirability of it.

Equipped with this information you can really set about planning the lessons you are going to teach. Of course you also need familiarity with the content of what you will teach, and the appropriate methods. That is inevitably subject-specific, but there are several elements of lesson planning that apply equally to German and Gymnastics, History or Home Economics.

## 7.2  Lesson planning

Lesson planning is commonly considered in terms of the didactic content of the lesson, in other words from the point of view of communicating the subject matter intended for the lesson. So teachers' manuals or course guides help the teacher set out material so that it can be learnt. From every point of view this is very important. If the content of a lesson is unintelligible, it is a waste of everybody's time. Also an unintelligible lesson is likely to be a disrupted lesson. Planning the sequence of elements to make sense of a topic reduces disruption.

### a)  General points in anti-disruption planning

There are some additional general points that will help your anti-disruption lesson planning.

- Have a clear *aim* to the lesson.
- Plan for the *full* length of the lesson. Have *reserves* available in case you have underestimated how long it all takes.
- Plan the tasks so that they are of a *length* and *variety* that children with *poor concentration* can handle.
- Make sure there is scope for pupils to succeed, whatever their academic level.
- Make sure the necessary *materials* are available and working.
- Make sure that the children have *access* to the materials otherwise some groups will become bored.
- Try to arrange the material so that the children feel that they have an element of *choice within clearly defined limits*, for instance, let them choose the sequence in which they attempt work.

It will be noted that none of these is in conflict with the planning of lessons for didactic purposes. This can be taken further. Planning lessons to reduce disruption represents good lesson planning generally. This is for two reasons. First it concentrates on attuning the lesson to the needs of the pupils in every respect, and this has to be a prime aim of lesson planning. Secondly anti-disruption planning is necessary to make any sense of pure content planning. In a disrupted classroom the best sequenced lesson content will not be learned by the pupils.

To this end there is one additional principle for lesson planning.

Leave some scope for flexibility.

A rigidly planned lesson can easily be blown off course and founder. A lesson planned so that the teacher can respond to the developing situation and select the best of a series of available systems is less likely to go so seriously wrong.

In addition to these general points there are specific elements that need to be considered in anti-disruption lesson planning.

## b)  Written materials and instructions

The written materials and instructions of the lesson make up the backbone of the lesson task. It is essential that they are clear and intelligible to *all* the pupils.

The intelligibility of written material can be greatly increased by applying a few rules. These are discussed in detail in the book on learning difficulties in this series, so are only summarised here.

Take account of these factors in constructing your own materials. They all affect the intelligibility of written materials.

| | |
|---|---|
| **Typeface** | Italic type is less readable than Roman type. Lower case is easier to read than upper case. |
| **Spacing** | Double spacing increases readability. |
| **Layout** | Generously set out pages increases readability. |
| **Active sentences** | Sentences written in active form (e.g. 'Tom shut the door') are easier to understand than passive sentences ('The door was shut by Tom'). |
| **Positivity** | Positive instructions (e.g. 'Keep the water boiling') are easier to follow than negative ones ('Do not allow the water temperature to drop below boiling point'). |
| **Headings** | Text is easier to read if broken up with headings. |
| **Diagrams** | Using diagrams and charts makes facts easier to group than the equivalent number of words. |
| **Advance organisers and summaries** | Summaries at beginning and end of the text help pupils recall the content. |

## c)  Pacing

The pacing of the lesson is vitally important to ensure maximum learning and minimum disruption.

- Plan the pacing of your lessons to take account of pupils' needs.
- Too fast and the pupils who are struggling will founder, fail, and be liable to disruption.
- Too slow and the work becomes boring, repetitious and devalued.

With the mixtures of ability found in any class, these constraints make for problems. The well planned lesson includes scope for the fast working higher achieving pupils to move on to work on interesting additional aspects of a topic, while slower workers are mastering the essential points. The well paced lesson moves pupils on to enable this spectrum of achievement. Flexibility, mentioned above, is perhaps best illustrated in terms of the pacing of the lesson. Pupils should only be moved on as they succeed, not to meet a pre-planned schedule. Inevitably this requires the teacher to be aware of, and respond to the behaviour of the pupils.

## d) Groupings

For most tasks it is possible to group the pupils in different ways. These can best be thought of as being:

- whole class work;
- group work;
- individual work.

Clearly the grouping relates to the task and the materials to be used. However the form of grouping has important implications, as our research has shown.

### Whole class work

This is essentially the traditional format of the teacher talking to the entire class. The likely consequences of this format are as follows:

1. The teacher can keep a close eye on all the pupils and may feel personally more secure for this reason.

2. There is likely to be *less* misbehaviour, but ...

3. Any misbehaviour that does occur is serious because the entire class will be aware of it, and everybody's work will be stopped. For this reason it is disruptive and ...

4. There have to be a large number of rules in operation, so more types of behaviour will draw the teacher's displeasure, particularly any social contact between pupils.

5. It is possible to communicate a large number of facts to a large number of people in a short time and it stresses both the task in hand, and the fact that the teacher is in charge, but ...

6. Pupil's attention is likely to wander, their learning in this situation is poor because they are essentially passive.

### Individual work

Individual work can take many forms. If the pupils are expected to work quietly on their own, the effect, in terms of the consequences of disruption, often resembles whole class work. However there are some additional points to remember:

1. Individual work gets every pupil involved and actively working. However ...

2. For less able pupils, or those with less self-esteem, being solely responsible for their work puts high expectations on them, and this is very anxiety provoking (see Chapter 5). Probably for this reason …

3. Misbehaviour is more frequent in this setting than in whole class teaching and as in whole class teaching …

4. Misbehaviour that occurs is serious and leads to disruption because everybody's attention will be focussed on it.

5. Again a large number of rules have to be in operation, most specifically barring contact between pupils.

---

**Group work**

In group work some of these problems are resolved, but others appear.

1. More misbehaviour is likely to occur than in whole class work but …

2. Misbehaviour that does occur is less serious in group work because the pupils are less focussed, and fewer rules need to apply. However …

3. It is hard for the teacher to monitor the behaviour of pupils: they have more autonomy than in other settings, and have more scope for misbehaviour.

4. More time is spent by pupils socialising and it is easier for the teacher to make social contact with pupils in group settings.

5. Less time is spent by pupils working when they are organised in groups but …

6. The quality of work is likely to be higher, particularly original, imaginative work, and the work of more anxious pupils is likely to be better. This is probably because learning is active, and the permitted social contact makes for a less anxiety producing situation.

---

From the summary of the effects of different groupings, it can be seen that none is perfect. Each serves a purpose. The best combination probably consists of using them in the following way.

**Whole class work.** This can be useful for control of excessive socialisation. Class work orientates everybody towards the task and the work of the lesson, and is best used at intervals for that purpose, moving work on, giving fairly brief specific instructions and re-stating rules.

**Group work.** This is the best format for pupils' active working. Permitted socialisation makes this the least stressful setting, but it has to be kept in check. The teacher must ensure that groups do not get stuck in the work, or distracted from it, and work has to be carefully structured and presented.

**Individual work.** Expectations of individual work by group members can ensure the engagement of pupils who are reluctant to work. This avoids the anxiety-generating format of everybody being expected to work solo.

## e) Planned groups

Your knowledge of the peer relationships of the class may well suggest that particular combinations of pupils are productive or counter-productive. With older pupils the attempt to dictate who shall work with whom frequently leads to trouble. However some manipulation of group membership may be possible if done carefully.

Covert group manipulation is however possible, and restricting the size of groups is a very effective way of doing so. Large groups (7 or more) rarely achieve much work, so groups of 3–4 are often the best, and it is unlikely that too many such groups will be disruptive.

## f) Classroom layout

Bearing in mind your observations of the school's approach to classroom management and the constraints of your allotted classroom, you can decide how you are going to organise the layout.

Points to bear in mind in considering classroom layout are these:

**Movement** is a potent instigator of disruption. Some movement is often inevitable, but locating needed materials so that there is a scrum to get them, or so that each pupil must go gathering from all round the room is asking for trouble. Pre-assembled sets of materials and well signposted collection points can greatly reduce the milling around.

**Re-organisation** often breeds trouble. At such times, for instance when switching from book-work to watching a video, there is no clear task for pupils, and a general state of chaos is likely to develop. The greater the re-organisation called for, the longer the chaos is likely to last. The pupils' feelings of passivity can be reduced if they are given warning of transitions beforehand.

**Group provision.** If you are planning for the pupils to work in groups for part of the time, it is useful to plan where groups will work. For each group to have a table or other work surface to work round increases the amount of work done in groups generally, so plan group sizes with this provision in mind.

## g) Providing essential materials

Most schools have a rule that pupils must equip themselves with necessary materials for work. Many problems arise because of the pupils who fail to do so. This offers the teacher a choice of actions. Make an issue out of it or provide the missing materials. By accumulating a collection of spare pens, pencils, rulers, crayons etc., it is possible to defuse these problems and keep the lesson going. When the pupil is working, or when the pencil is returned, is the time for a reminder that next time he should bring his own.

## h) Keeping track of materials

In any lesson where materials are handed out to pupils for the duration of the lesson, it is the teacher's job to keep track of them. Considerable chaos and aggravation may be avoided by doing so efficiently. Some suggestions may help.

- Be sure that you know how many of each item you handed out. Let the pupils know when you hand items out that you have counted them, and expect the same number returned. This can avoid quite a lot of temptation and argument.
- Leave time in your lesson plan for gathering in loaned materials.
- For particularly significant items, make identified individuals responsible for the loan not just the group or the class generally.

## i) Learn to predict

It is worth trying to predict whether certain elements of a planned lesson will generate trouble.

Plan your response to predictable problems as in the following examples:

- It is a fair bet that provision of syringes for the accurate dispersing of liquids in science practicals will lead to them being used as water pistols.
- It is a fair bet that quite a bit of adolescent smirking will accompany the lines in *The Lady of Shallot* that go:
    'The mirror crack'd from side to side;
    "The curse is come upon me", cried
    The Lady of Shallot.'
- Magnets are such fun, and so attractive that they will be applied to a 'friend's' watch, and are highly liable to disappear – simply not get handed back in at the end of a lesson using them.

With forethought, you can plan a response to these problems.

## 7.3 Conclusion

Equipped with this information, and with a lesson planned with these points in mind, you will be prepared to meet your pupils.

As was mentioned at the beginning of this chapter, the full battery of advice offered may be daunting, but the intention is to offer as complete a set as possible to cover the field. There should be no inference that every one of these suggestions has to be followed through for success. However every one can be useful and could help to reduce problems.

In a really badly planned lesson all types of disruption are likely. Unfortunately the opposite is not entirely true; even in a really well planned lesson disruption may occur, but at least the most predictable causes can be prevented, and provision can be made for dealing with other possible problems.

# Preventing disruption

## 8.1 Introduction – teachers' behaviour

One of the major trends in modern medicine, dentistry and social work is away from 'cure' towards 'prevention'. The prevention of disruption covers a vast field. Almost any good teaching can be thought of as preventing disruption. Planning lessons so that pupils do not become bored, frustrated or over-anxious will prevent disruption as will intervening so as to minimise the escalation of problems. These two aspects are considered in Chapters 7 and 9 respectively, but between the two lies the prevention of disruption by the general behaviour of the teacher in the classroom.

It is very clear from watching lessons that the behaviour of the teacher has an effect on the pupils' behaviour. It would be strange if this were not the case, but it does give the teacher an important tool for preventing disruption and maximising the positive aspects of lessons.

In order to use this with the greatest efficiency, it is particularly important to understand the phenomenon of disruption. This was discussed in Chapter 5, but a brief summary seems useful here.

---

- Behaviour that leads to disruption arises essentially from the insecurity of the pupil.
- A prime source of that insecurity is frustration especially that stemming from a mismatch between the external expectations made of the pupil and his internal self evaluation.
- The two prime areas for such mismatch are the task and the social dimensions that make up the predominant agenda of the classroom.

---

This analysis of disruption is particularly important in understanding the influence of the classroom behaviour of the teacher on that of the pupil. This will be discussed under a series of headings.

## 8.2 General points

### a) Balance

As the teacher, it is your task to establish the balance between the two aspects of the classroom agenda, *work* and *social contact*.

Undue emphasis on the work element has two direct effects. First it makes the work less satisfying (Hollander, 1978) and secondly it makes social contact illegal, or attempts to do so. To achieve this you would have to bring into force a large and ever expanding set of rules; a dangerous situation that will be considered below.

Over-emphasis on the social part of the agenda devalues the work. It is important to remember that the work is the primary purpose of the school. Other functions could be performed better elsewhere, perhaps in a youth club for instance. Pupils also feel this to be the case, and chatting is seen as a waste of time.

## b) Reasonable expectations

The anxiety-provoking effect of making excessive demands on pupils was mentioned above, and discussed in Chapter 5. As a teacher your role is to have expectations of a pupil's performance and behaviour, to make demands on the pupil.

> You must recognise each pupil's starting point, his self-esteem or self-image, and your expectations must relate to that starting point.

This conflict between self-esteem and expectation is significant both in terms of the pupil's work and his social functioning. Specific suggestions in these two dimensions will be made in the following sections, but it is important to remember the interactions of these two aspects.

## c) Rules and commands

An enormous number and range of rules can apply in a classroom, and they regulate the behaviour of the pupils. However there are two problems with regulating all behaviour with rules.

First, infringement of rules is the quick route to a confrontation, in fact some authors (for instance Hargreaves *et al.,* op.cit.) view confrontation in terms of rule breaking and responses to that. The problem is that the teacher's response to a pupil who has broken a rule is inevitably negative. Telling off, challenging or otherwise criticising a person is always something of a threat, but if the pupil feels inadequate and unable to cope with adults, the threat to his self-esteem is massive. A socially insecure person easily feels threatened, and such a feeling makes most people defend themselves. This is a reasonable description of an escalating disruptive incident.

Secondly, rules work both ways. The teacher who lays down the rule 'No talking' puts a clear expectation on the pupils that they will not talk. But that teacher also puts on him or herself the corresponding expectation of responding to all infringements of the rule. Failure to do so is clearly unfair so both the rule and the teacher lose all credibility. It and he merely appear arbitrary. Unpredictably applied rules also create the problem that the pupils do not know where they stand. Such uncertainty is as potent a force generating anxiety as is the conflict of self-image discussed above. Once a rule is in place the teacher is damned either way.

> Minimise the numer of rules but state and explain them clearly. This is not to lower standards, merely to reduce the number of injunctions that carry the supposed authority to the teacher.

## d) Requests and explanations

> Generally phrase commands in the form of requests, with an explanation.

The difference between an ex cathedra rule and a request is enormous. By requesting a pupil to do something, and giving an explanation for the request, you do two things.

First, your behaviour is acting as a creditable model for behaviour. The pupil is given the recognition that he is important enough to merit being given an explanation for why a particular thing is asked of him. His self-esteem is not undermined. He is not being threatened. The teacher is implicitly assuming that the pupil is reasonable and rational and generally has reasons for his own actions.

Secondly, although you can still pursue the matter if a request is ignored, you have more options open than if a command is disobeyed. There is less immediate loss of face, so less immediate risk of the confrontation escalating into serious disruption.

## e) Avoiding threats

> Avoid using threats.

Issuing a threat has all the disadvantages of a rule or command, but involves even more escalation. If the pupil disobeys, failure on your part to carry out a threat makes you appear really ridiculous and unpredictable.

Issuing a threat hands control for an interaction over to the pupil. He knows what can happen, and can decide whether it will or not, and such assumption of control is alarming to pupil as well as teacher. The result of such alarm or anxiety is likely to be an increase in the egocentricity of those involved (see Chapter 4), imputation of threatening motives to the other and escalation of trouble. There is an awful inevitability about threats.

## f) General volume of talk

> Do not shout. Do not whisper.

The overall loudness with which the teacher conducts the class has three effects.

First, the teacher's style sets the tone, or, more to the point, the volume control for the whole class as a group. If you, the teacher feel obliged to increase your volume so as to talk above the noise of the class, the pupils are highly likely to do the same, and very soon everybody will be shouting.

Secondly, if your general level of talking is quite low, the occasional loud comment, at times of danger ('Put that Sulphuric Acid **down**') or trouble ('Sit down Michael! **Now!**') will really carry some weight.

Thirdly, talking loudly is generally perceived as being aggressive. Talking relatively quietly, it is easier to appear positive and friendly, in other words to be responding to pupils as individuals rather than as a herd.

That said, the really quiet teacher can totally fail to communicate either the work content of the lesson or the teacher's position as being in charge of the class. Being too quiet, or too loud, is often perceived as a lack of confidence, which makes the class, and especially its insecure members, feel even less secure.

## g) Clarity

In the introduction to this chapter, the understanding of disruption reached in Chapter 5 was summarised. Central to that argument was the idea that both misbehaviour and egocentricity (blaming the other peron) to a great extent resulted from anxiety. A prime source of anxiety is confusion, so it is the teacher's task to minimise confusion.

> Make yourself clear.

In addition clarity has to be in the pupil's understanding, not merely in the teacher's explanations, so it is often necessary to repeat and rephrase things in order to be clearly understood.

It is also implicit from the introduction that clarity has to apply in both aspects of your behaviour; work and social contact. Clarity in terms of work is relatively easy to describe, and comes largely from clear lesson planning and presentation. If you have some definite purpose to the lesson's work it is likely to be communicated to the pupils.

Clarity in social contact may appear less understandable. Perhaps the best example of this is the confusion produced by shouting a comment to a child the far side of the room 'Better work; best thing you have done this term'. Here the content appears positive, but the form of delivery – shouting and the impossibility of accompanying the compliment with the slight smile that makes a compliment sincere – can make it appear negative. The conflict between the two makes for a lack of clarity that is confusing at a personal level. To a pupil who is not skilled at understanding the process of social contact this confusion is quite stressful, and the undesirable aspects of stress have been discussed quite fully above.

## h) Being and appearing pleasant

It has often been said that liking children helps in being a teacher. It is difficult to train teachers to like children, but it has been shown in several other spheres (Trower *et al.*, 1978) that giving the impression of liking other people generally makes them like you more and therefore be more likeable. This may sound a bit devious, but appearing to like people really can help. Perhaps it is more apparent that the opposite, being aggressive to pupils and generally seeming to dislike them is not associated with good behaviour (Gray, 1987).

It is not easy to describe ways of appearing pleasant towards pupils because it tends to appear cloying. However positive response to acceptable or desired behaviour is far more effective than attempts to stop unwanted behaviour with negative approaches.

- Smile at pupils.
- Nod when they tell you something.
- Look at them.
- Listen to them.
- Be prepared to be physically near to them.
- In short, be attentive.

These tactics are spontaneously 'employed' by teachers who do actually respect, and even like, their pupils, but the process can work the other way too. The success of these tactics leads to greater liking and respect by the teacher of the pupils, and vice versa. It is a virtuous, rather than vicious, circle.

It is easier to itemise behaviours which make the teacher appear to dislike pupils. Shouting, staring, frowning and keeping at a distance from the pupil all tend to be seen as signals that the pupil is disliked. It is threatening for a pupil to feel disliked and that generates great anxiety.

## i)  Being human

The principal suggested root of pupil misbehaviour was anxiety, and one of the self-perpetuating aspects of that was seen as the egocentric view point that blames the other person. Blaming the other person often takes the form of labelling him, and then the one dimentional label serves as the picture of the person.

A very effective way of dispelling or defusing labels is to demonstrate that you are human. Attempts to appear *totally* competent divorce you from humanity and the label seems an adequate representation.

- Ask for help when you clearly need it.
- Apologise for mistakes or failures.
- Admit to problems.
  All these things will make you appear human, and labels will not fit so well. So a comment such as 'I'm afraid it will take me a while to learn all your names' is obviously true when you first meet a class; it also shows you to be human.

The other importance of these admissions is that they make the relationship between teacher and pupils much more even. The examples given above (asking for help, apologising and admitting to problems) are major elements of what a teacher expects a pupil to do. Most of the contact between pupil and teacher is expected to be on the basis of the pupil making these statements of failure and asking the teacher's help. By occasionally doing the same, you are making these acts more acceptable, and serve as a good model for how to behave in such circumstances.

# 8.3  Scanning

In addition to the general classroom skills of a teacher, described above, there is one skill, that needs to be exercised at all times, and that is scanning. It is by the use of scanning that the good teacher appears to know what is going on behind his back, and in every other part of the class, all the time.

## a) The importance of scanning

Kounin's research (1970) showed that disruption was minimal, and work maximal where a teacher exhibited two skills identified with the wonderful terminology of 'With-it-ness' and 'Overlappingness'. Teachers were scored high on the 'With-it-ness' rating if they:

- Intervened with the correct pupil.
- Intervened with the more serious of the simultaneous misbehaviours.
- Intervened before the misbehaviour spread.
- Intervened before the misbehaviour became serious.

'Overlappingness' is to a considerable extent the way in which the teacher achieves 'With-it-ness', when confronted with two matters, both of which demand the teacher's attention. The teacher shows 'overlappingness' by attending to both simultaneously.

These findings all make intuitive sense. You can reduce disruption by intervening accurately and early in a disruptive incident. The chances of doing so are increased by responding to what is going on all over the classroom, and influencing behaviour in more than one place at a time (overlapping). To do this requires two things. Keeping a look out, and knowing what to look for.

## b) The process of scanning

The actual process of scanning consists of continually watching the pupils.

**A**

- In talking to a whole class, look at one pupil for a sentence or so, then at another, in another part of the class. This monitors the whole class, and lets the pupils know that they are being monitored.
- In talking to an individual or group, divide your time between looking at the pupil you are talking to (which is normal good manners) and checking other pupils.

This makes you resemble a radar unit, continually monitoring what is happening, hence the term scanning.

## c) Warning signals

It is really not very useful keeping a close look-out without consciously knowing what to look (and listen) out for.

Look out for these warning signals.

**1. Pitch of sound.** You have to get familiar with the working buzz of a particular class. Changes in the buzz often signal trouble, so an increase in giggling or whispering warns you of misbehaviour.

**2. Volume of noise.** Trouble usually involves making a noise so it is worth responding to the general volume of sound. Occasionally misbehaviour will be accompanied by silence, but it is worth checking that a silence is not the quiet of pupils really working.

**3. Speed of movement.** Trouble often comes at a run, so check on pupils who seem to be in a hurry.

**4. Checking on the teacher.** Pupils who are working individually or in groups rarely look towards the teacher. Where this happens it suggests trouble.

**5. Non-work groupings.** In lessons where the pupils are allowed to move about, knots of pupils sometimes develop, drawing members of several work groups. Such gatherings are rarely in the teacher's interests.

Alerted to signals such as these the early intervention of the teacher is possible. Forms and techniques of intervention are discussed in Chapter 9, but early intervention, and letting the pupils know that they are being monitored are the best ways of preventing misbehaviour escalating into disruption.

# 8.4 Specific recommendations for phases of a lesson

The other recommendations that stem from understanding disruption are best considered in relation to the different phases of the lesson. Lessons have been differently divided into phases (for example, Laslett and Smith, 1984; Hargreaves *et al.*, 1975) but the classical division of drama into *beginning*, *middle* and *end* seems the most fundamental. In addition to the general recommendations above, specific recommendations apply to these phases. In each phase the two major agenda items (work and social) have to be considered in addition to more specific aspects.

## a) Beginning

### *Punctuality*

Arrive on time and start the lesson on time.

Arriving on time enables you to get straight into the driving seat, and prevents any of the children taking control of the group. More prosaically, it enables you to stop the inevitable messing around before it develops into serious trouble. Additionally it enables you to gauge the general feeling of the class, and to get everything prepared.

Being in the classroom before the pupils arrive enables you to admit the pupils to *your* classroom, with the implication that it is on your terms (Marland, 1975).

### Social agenda

The teacher can really set the social tone for the entire lesson at the beginning.

- Greet the pupils as they arrive, or, better, in the corridor before you admit them to the classroom. It is best to chat at this stage but to show disapproval of any unacceptable behaviour. Be especially sure to greet any potential disrupters at this stage by name, and make a point of talking to them.
- Make it clear to the pupils at the beginning what behaviour you are prepared to tolerate. e.g. 'I do not mind you talking while you do this work, but if it gets too noisy it's difficult to concentrate, so keep the noise down.'
- Give them a bit of time to settle down, and use this time to continue the business of greeting and talking.

### Work agenda

As with the social aspect of the lesson, the tone for the work is set at the beginning.

- Introduce the work of the lesson. Make it seem important and as interesting as you can.
- Tell the pupils what is expected of them in terms of work for the whole lesson e.g. 'Ten minutes before the end of the lesson we will be looking at a film strip on tooth decay, so make sure you have finished your food tests before then'.

The first work usually consists of giving an introduction to the lesson content to the whole class (see Chapter 7 Grouping). If this is brief it can serve to set the tone, and standards for the lesson in a positive way. If this introduction becomes extended it can make for a boring start to the work, and sow the seeds of trouble.

The first piece of active work for the pupils should be something they can succeed at. Failure and frustration at the beginning of the lesson is hard to counter later on. Also failure in the first task often makes later work unintelligible, especially if the work is in any way sequential. This is the basis of recommendations (Laslett and Smith, 1984) to start with a small piece of work involving reinforcement of items previously learned, in which all the pupils can succeed. It is possible to move pupils on from it once they have finished this work, and by then most of the confusions of the lesson's start (lost pens, late pupils or impending music lessons) have been resolved.

## b) Middle

The middle of the lesson is the meat of it when the purposes of the lesson can be achieved. However it is still vital to remember the twin agendas of the lesson – work and social.

# Work agenda

> Work is the main purpose. You must make it important, and make it clear
> that it is important.

For the pupils to work and learn is clearly the intention of a lesson. Our own
research has shown that pupils work more when the teacher concentrates on
work. This is not surprising, but it does clearly put the onus on the teacher to
emphasise the importance of the work in hand.

The ways in which the teacher emphasises the work have also been
investigated in detail, especially by Kounin (1970) and Brophy and Evertson
(1976). However attaching importance to work should not be seen as an
alternative to the social agenda of the lesson (see below) nor are the two in
conflict.

Kounin's lesson observation related both deviant behaviour and work
involvement to the teacher's behaviour. It is very detailed, but some of the
outstanding findings should be borne in mind by practising teachers generally.

Predictably Kounin found that what encouraged pupils to work also
reduced disruption. Two specific elements of the teacher's behaviour were
related to the pupils' work. These were called 'Smoothness' and
'Momentum'.

**Smoothness** was defined rather negatively in terms of the absence from the
teacher's behaviour of actions that interfered with the flow of work. It might
appear strange to think of the teacher interfering with work, but Kounin
found these actions to be common, and significant in generating disruption.

The detailed acts that reduced the 'smoothness' of the lesson were
identified in the following rather splendid terminology.

**1. Stimulus-boundedness.** This is when the teacher pays attention to an
irrelevant intrusive detail ignoring, interrupting and undermining the work in
hand ('Who left a piece of paper on the floor?').

**2. Thrusts.** This is when the teacher bursts in on the pupil's work with an
unrelated question or instruction.

**3. Dangles.** This is when the teacher is engaged in a demonstration, giving an
instruction etc. and leaves it hanging in mid air – to pursue it later ('Look at
the ... has anybody seen my pen? ... the chart on page 46').

**4. Truncations.** These are like dangles, but the thread is never picked up
again.

**5. Flip-flops.** These are when the teacher stops pupils in one activity, starts a
second, and then gets everybody to return to the first ('Put away your
worksheets and watch the O.H.P. screen. Check your answer to question 6 on
the worksheet').

**Momentum.** In addition to these five assaults on the smoothness of the
lesson there were two other failings that produced a reduction in the
'momentum' of the lesson. These did not stop or interrupt the work, they
simply made it progress steadily but very, very slowly. They were:

**1. Overdwelling.** This consists of giving unnecessarily minute detailed instructions ('On a clean page put the date, underline it. Now draw a margin. Put the heading and the number 1 in the margin').

**2. Fragmentation.** This involves dealing with individuals one after another when the entire group could be asked simultaneously ('All of you sit down. Now Chris come and get your book. Now you Wayne. Now come and get yours Hannah .....'). There might be understandable reasons for doing this, but the effect is to fragment the lesson.

All these detailed actions by the teacher were related to reduction in the amount of work done, and increase in the disruption.

It is not hard to see intuitively that this should be the result but it is useful to relate it to the ideas developed in this book.

Every one of these actions undermines the emphasis or validity of the claim that the work of the lesson is important. In each case something else is clearly more important than the task of learning the lesson contents. This generates frustration, a conflict of motivations, anxiety and predictably, this leads to misbehaviour and disruption. Emphasis on work by the teacher is a major factor reducing disruption.

**Transitions.** The concept of 'smoothness' was also used by Brophy and Evertson (1976), but they employed the word slightly differently. For them it was about the transition of work from one activity to another. The keys to success in doing this lay in having varied activities and plenty of materials.

Transition from one activity to another has also been identified as a danger point by Hargreaves *et al.* (1975). In any sequence of behaviour, the changeover point from one activity to another is a point when distraction is most probable. The key to avoiding problems appears to be to use the work-related techniques outlined above for starting a lesson. So it is essential to make clear the teacher's intentions behind the work, and the detailed expectations the teacher has of the pupils. Transitions are also times when there is a hiccup in the work agenda. The pupils will tend to fill that gap with other activities and so become more social, chatter and so on. This is inevitable, so giving them some scope for it can reduce confrontations.

Make clear transition from one activity to the next. Give pupils warning that they will have to work a transition. Ensure that the new activity is ready for the pupils.

**Teaching the whole class.** One more of Kounin's measures of teacher performance is also worth describing in the present context. It was 'Group Alerting'. This consisted in essence of keeping all the pupils attending and on their toes. This is clearly a major part of teaching the entire class. It is best illustrated in a talk and question situation. If you precede the question with a pupil's name, then the rest of the class know they can ignore you. Consistently addressing a limited section of the class, or asking questions in a regular, predetermined way has the same effect.

In questioning, ask the question first, then select who is to answer. The choice of who is to answer should depend on the difficulty of the question. Open-ended questions can help the more able pupils to expand the work.

## Social agenda

The social aspects of the main part of the lesson were briefly mentioned above as *not* being in conflict with the work emphasis. It is possible to show that work is important while remaining pleasant to the pupils.

**Praise.**   The most closely linked aspect is the use of praise. Praise for good work, or any acceptable behaviour is far more likely to improve behaviour then criticism or censure for unwanted behaviour. However praise must always be perceived as such by the pupil. Repetitious routine praise can easily become dull, hollow, and worthless so, as Laslett and Smith (1984) point out, a range of synonyms for 'good' is useful. Certainly the more expressive the words used, the more likely it is that praise be seen as being of value.

> Remember to praise pupils who quietly get on with their work. They are on your side and you must keep them there.

**Individual contact.**   An additional element in the act of praising a pupil is that praise has to be given almost in confidence. Public praise can often be two-edged, more embarrassing than encouraging.

Other personal contact also tends to be invalidated if it is conducted in public. This is really only to emphasise that pupils have much the same feelings as any other people, and dislike discussing matters of an even slightly personal nature in public.

> To make any personal contact with a pupil, you must be near to him, and respect his privacy.

Certain situations in lessons are far better suited to personal contact than others. So beginnings and ends of lessons are usually sufficiently fluid to make contact possible. In addition it is usually possible to talk relatively quietly with individuals during group-work sessions. This is because at such times the teacher is not the controller of the detailed actions of pupils, so there is less of an audience for the conversation.

Such conversations with pupils are essentially like conversations with anybody else, and must not take the form of an interview. Extracting information from a pupil is not likely to make him feel that you care about him as a person. Talking at this sort of level involves discussion, and sharing. So preferences as to football teams, music, shops, clothes and so on can constitute the basis of such conversations, as long as it is a process of give and take. But don't overdo such topics as this may undermine work (see 8.2 and below) and don't try to be 'one of the boys'. This is not your actual, nor your expected role.

**Avoiding sidetracks.**   The happy chatting described in the previous section constitutes an element of the personal social recognition of individual pupils. However, for many pupils this process can become the preferred activity to working. It is your role therefore to draw the balance between the two. The methods for preventing the social element of the class agenda getting to predominate are much the same as the methods used to bring any other conversation politely to a halt.

Bring sidetracking chatting sessions to an end with phrases such as:

- 'Interesting, we must talk about it later.'
- 'Well we must get on with some work now.'
- 'Excuse me I must go and deal with Michael.'

Each of these carries the desired message that the discussion, and therefore the person, is important, but that at the moment work is the order of the day.

**Names.** Knowing a pupil's name is one clear way of showing that he is a recognised individual. Incidentally it also makes it much easier to control the pupil in the event of misbehaviour. Several tricks can help in remembering names.

- Use seating plans with names on.
- Use associations between the name and the physical appearance of a pupil as a private reminder.
- Hand materials to pupils and use names as you do so. This also shows you which names you still need to learn.
- Use the pupil's name when writing comments on work, 'Good work Michael' is more positive than just 'Good work'.
- Use pupils' names in talking to them generally, do not just keep them for emergencies.

## c) End

Structure at the end of a lesson is all too easily lost in a sigh of relief that it is nearly over. However, trouble at the end of the lesson can still be serious. For one thing, the pupils leaving one lesson are not vanishing into limbo, they are usually going to another lesson, and you owe it to your colleague to leave the pupils in the state in which you would hope to receive them.

At a more personal level, your end of one lesson with a particular class is the background to your next lesson with that class even if that is next week. It is also your personal background to the lesson you are just about to start, and your personal stress, carried from one lesson is likely to prejudice your performance in the next. So, bringing lessons to a successful conclusion really does matter.

### Timing, organisation and materials

The amount of time needed for clearing up and ending a lesson depends above all on the materials that have to be sorted out. A full-scale laboratory practical is bound to take longer than a lesson where pupils are doing creative writing in their books. However even in that latter case, time must be allowed for them to finish off a sentence or paragraph. Marland (1975) suggests that three minutes should be allowed for cleaning up and collecting materials. Clearly this is too rigid, in the light of the differences between lessons, but a business-like ending to the lesson is definitely important. Rutter *et al.* (1979) showed this to be the case in London schools with their demonstrated association between disruptive behaviour and the proportion of lessons that ended early. The use of very ritualised controls for the end of lessons ('Sitting still in silence with arms folded') can act as a routine for smaller children, but is likely to lead to more confrontations than it is worth with older ones.

However the instruction 'Sit down when you finish clearing up, then I'll know when everybody is ready', can bring the clearing up to a relatively placid conclusion. Finally, the teacher standing by the door as the pupils leave has the opportunity both to prevent a scrum in the doorway, and to say good-bye to pupils.

In addition to the organisational tasks of the end of the lesson, the teacher needs to consider the tasks to be achieved in relation to the work and the personal agendas.

## Work agenda

In relation to the work of the lesson there are three distinct tasks to be achieved before the pupils depart.

**Completion.** It considerably devalues work being done by a pupil if he is stopped working in mid-sentence or in the middle of a task. Clearly the task is unimportant if stopping for lunch takes precedence.

> Give pupils warning of the end of the lesson; the larger the individual tasks, the longer the warning needed, but something like a five-minute warning is always a good idea. It also helps the pupil to plan, which has to be one of the long-term aims of school.

**Consolidation.** It is important to allow time for this.

> Towards the end of a lesson consolidate the work done. This may be just a reminder of points covered, but it may involve relating the minutiae of a task to the principal it was intended to illustrate.

In very individualised work, or open-ended investigations it may be difficult to do this with the entire class, but it is still worth doing with the individual work groups.

**Feed-back.** This gives pupils a guide-line as to what you expect of them, and reduces misunderstandings. Direct, clear and straightforward feedback makes it possible for a pupil to assess his performance.

> Give some indication of how you felt individuals have worked and behaved.

In this context it is wise to make feedback as positive as possible, so at best it can be phrased in terms of straight praise. If however praise is really not possible, feedback can be in terms of 'I know you can do better than you have. I'm sure you will do better next time'. This is direct without doing damage to the pupil's self-esteem. He should not depart feeling that he is useless, but knowledge that his performance was not acceptable is necessary if he is to modify it.

In this way, direct feedback can reduce the pupil's insecurity. He knows what the teacher thinks he is capable of, and knows how his performance related to that. This can reduce his anxiety about work given to him in future.

**Preparation.** Preparation for future work can stem directly out of the consolidation of past work.

> Give pupils some indication of what is intended for the next lesson as another way of involving them in the work, making them less passive.

At its least positive end, preparing may border on repairing. So, if a lesson has not been well received or the pupils have found the work difficult, it is well worth indicating that next time they will be doing something a bit different.

### Social agenda

The social tasks of the end of the lesson are essentially comparable to those related to the work. The teacher has been in a social setting with the pupils, and such contact has to be brought to an end. The end of the lesson provides a good opportunity for talking to pupils, showing them that you are interested in them as people, and that you value contact with them. In addition to using the repertoire of skills suggested for ending conversations with pupils during the lesson, it is important so say good-bye at the end of a lesson.

# 8.5 Conclusion

The main weapons in the teacher's armoury for the prevention of disruption are the planning of lessons and the teacher's own classroom behaviour. The key to both is the recognition of the importance of the twin elements of the classroom agenda, the work and the social components. The good teacher is aware of the beneficial effects of success, and the dangers of disruption that arise from a pupil cornered by the anxiety of uncertainty. Such stress can most easily come from disparity between external expectations and self-image in either work or the social dimensions, and minimising these is the teacher's task.

Unfortunately, in even the best planned and executed lesson, there are other sources of conflict for pupils, and disruption can result from these. Controlling the escalation of such problems is an essential skill for the good teacher, and the next chapter considers the interventions that can be used.

# ▌Intervention

## 9

# Aims of intervention

The preceding two chapters describe and discuss methods that a teacher can use to prevent or minimise misbehaviour. However no such set of suggestions can ever hope to stop pupils misbehaving entirely, so teachers do need to intervene.

It seems obvious, but worth recognising that the teacher's aim in intervention is twofold. First he or she wants to stop the misbehaviour and return pupils to the work expected of them. Secondly and more defensively, the teacher wants to prevent the problem escalating either with the involvement of other pupils, or with the development of a confrontation between pupil and teacher. Both of these aims are worth considering.

## a) Return to work

In aiming to return pupils to the work expected of them, you need to bear in mind the possible influence of that work in generating the problem in the first place. If a pupil who is feeling anxious about doing a piece of work, gets the instruction 'Get on with your work!' it can only heighten that anxiety. To this extent, the teacher does need to view misbehaviour as something of a criticism of the lesson.

This then puts the onus on you, the teacher, to do something about the problem. Clearly this can be at two levels: short-term and long-term. In the short-term, many of the intervention techniques described below are aimed at reducing problems with the work, emphasising the importance of the work, and showing the pupil that there is not a conflict between the expectations of work, and his ability.

In the long-term, you need to use information as to which lessons, or parts of lessons were disrupted, in future planning. As a form of criticism, disruption is rather blunt, but it does tell you how different topics or presentations were received, and when the task of engaging pupils' interest is particularly necessary.

## b) Preventing escalation

Almost inevitably, serious disruption comes about by a process of escalation (Pik, 1981). It is very unusual for serious trouble to erupt without a build-up.

By its very nature, the process of escalation involves increasing numbers of people, even if only in the capacity of an audience. This is so whether it is conflict between pupils or confrontation between a pupil and the teacher. So, whatever the origin of the problem, it develops into one in which the pupil's skills at relating to other people are called on.

In Chapter 2, the point was made that disruptive pupils tend to be poor at relating to others, particularly adults. For this reason, it is predictable that once such pupils become involved in a confrontation, they will be unable to scale it down. On the contrary, they are liable to escalate it. The more a person feels under threat, the more he feels he must defend himself, and defence can often be at the other's expense, so the escalation receives another twist.

Viewing the process of escalation in this way makes disruption understandable. Clearly, the early part of a disruptive incident may relate to either the work or the social aspects of the classroom agenda. The pupil misbehaves because of problems in one or both of these areas. If an incident escalates, it always moves into the area where personal relationships need to be considered and resolved.

In this context it is important to note that in our research (Gray *et al.*, 1986), almost all (19 out of 22) of the pupils identified as *seriously* disruptive in the sample had poor social skills with adults. This strongly supports the emphasis being placed on these skills in considering the process of escalation. Pupils are likely to be identified as seriously disruptive if their interactions with teachers tend to escalate, and the pupils for whom this is the case have poor social skills with adults.

It is also worth noting here that *all* the girls who were identified by staff as even somewhat disruptive had poor social skills, whereas quite a proportion of the boys (20 out of 52) did not, a finding that may throw light in two directions. On the one hand this may explain the often heard comment that 'difficult girls are really difficult'. On the other hand it may suggest that teachers' expectations of girls are that they should be 'nice and polite' (socially skilled), and those who are not so are seen as disruptive. By contrast it may be that a certain amount of rudeness is expected of boys, but they are expected to work; an idea supported by the fact that almost all the disruptive boys (44 out of 52) had low academic self-images. It was among the seriously disruptive boys that social skills problems were prevalent.

For these reasons it seems entirely reasonable to consider social skills problems as being central to the process of escalation, and as becoming increasingly important as an incident develops. Therefore, the way in which you, the teacher must intervene depends to a considerable extent on when you do so.

## 9.2  Style of intervention

This understanding of the process of escalation underlines the importance of the teacher's style of intervention. Serious escalation of a confrontation is essentially a duel (Pik, op.cit.) so if the teacher does not play his part, the escalation can be interrupted. The central element in escalation is the increasing anger and anxiety of both teacher and pupil, so the teacher has to try to reduce that stress. There are particular aspects to the teacher's style that can do this.

### a)  Minimising aggression

Rising aggression is characteristic of escalating confrontations, so the teacher can do a lot to defuse things by avoiding expressions of anger or aggression.

This is not to devalue giving the impression of authority. Shouting, staring, thumping the table and moving rapidly towards a pupil all convey the message of aggression, and such messages can easily slip over into appearing unpredictable and scared.

> Be calm, attentive and rational. These project the direct opposite of aggression, and will avoid exacerbating the pupils anxiety.

## b) Maximising clarity

> Make your interventions, your instructions or statements clear and unambiguous.

'Incoherent rage' is a familiar cliché and certainly a person who is really angry makes little sense. Clarity therefore contributes to the impression that the teacher is not angry while emphasising the position of authority. Lack of clarity has another effect. Confusion is a potent source of stress, and making confused comments, statements or instructions to a pupil only increases his stress. The result is that the problem gets worse, so in intervention, even more than during the rest of the lesson, clarity is essential.

## c) Humour

The most powerful defuser of anxiety can be humour. Laughing *at* a pupil during a confrontation further threatens his faltering self-esteem, but finding something else amusing shows that the teacher is feeling unthreatened, and is in control. This is really not a style to try for – forced humour is deadly – but nor is it something to suppress.

## d) Timing

> Intervene early.

In Chapter 8, the research of Kounin (1970) was referred to. In that work it was found that there was less disruption if the teacher intervened soon, when a pupil started to misbehave (teacher 'with-it-ness' in Kounin's terminology). Clearly early intervention in misbehaviour reduces disruption. Three reasons can be offered for this, derived from the ideas developed in Chapter 5.

**1.** The teacher who intervenes early gives the clear message that he is not frightened of the situation. Delay suggests ambivalence in the teacher. Anxiety stemming from ambivalence is easily detected by pupils, and communicated to them, exacerbating their own anxiety.

**2.** The longer a pupil persists in misbehaving, the more the validity of appropriate behaviour is called into doubt. If those expectations are uncertain, the whole situation becomes more unpredictable and anxious.

**3.** As outlined in the preceding section on escalation, delay in intervention involves increasing numbers of people. This in itself means that the disruption to the lesson is more serious than it might have been. It also increases the importance of the pupil's social skills, and this may well mean that the problem becomes more complicated.

The three (rather ponderous) explanations above all advocate early intervention in a disruptive incident. However one major point has to be made to qualify this.

Early intervention is not the same as fast or hasty intervention. If intervention is an instantaneous reflex action it is highly likely to be the wrong intervention. The brief pause between detecting a problem and intervening can be worth fine gold. In that pause you can assess the situation.

Points to consider are:
- How serious is the problem?
- How many pupils are involved already?
- Is their misbehaviour physically dangerous?
- Which pupil(s) should be talked to (first)?
- Is the pupil likely to find your approach threatening?
- Is the pupil likely to be finding the work threatening?

Some of this information can be picked up quickly from looking at what is going on, some relies on the teacher's knowledge of the pupils involved. All this information is needed in determining how to intervene, and detecting the problem early enables the teacher to intervene more appropriately.

The work of Brophy and Evertson (1976) supports this last point. They found that teachers who scanned (monitored) class activity frequently made fewer intervention errors. The errors that concerned the authors were 'target errors' (delaying an intervention or over-hasty and escalating intervention).

It is important, in terms of understanding disruption to note the similarity between these 'intervention errors' and the description in Chapter 5 of behaviour in conditions of stress. In that chapter, teacher stress was identified as generating egocentricity in attributing motives to pupils. Such narrowing of perspectives is also exemplified in these 'intervention errors'. The teacher under stress is less likely to be able to perceive the situation objectively, and that is essential to resolving the problem. However the very process of really scanning the class is a potent way of reducing the momentary panic produced by finding there is a problem. For this reason also, instant intervention can be the wrong intervention.

# 9.3  Techniques of intervention

The discussion above clearly points towards intervening in a considered way when misbehaviour occurs. Clearly the technique employed should depend on the situation, but the most important determinant has to be the severity of the situation. At any stage, there are four golden rules.

**Avoid doing these things:**
- Telling off the wrong child.
- Delaying intervention when disruption develops.
- Being unreasonably hard on petty misbehaviour.
- Using threats to either a single child or the whole class.

## a) Low-level problems

### Gesture

Just look at the child, shake your head, wag a finger or point at the work.

At its lowest level, intervention consists of simply reminding a pupil what is expected of him. Generally pupils know how they are meant to behave, and you the teacher represent that set of expectations. Reminding him of your presence reinforces these expectations. However there should be no anger, just a reminder. The implication is that the pupil is basically well behaved but just for a moment he forgot where he was and what he should be doing. A smile accompanying the gesture supports the message.

## Proximity

Get near the child. Do this gently, slowly and without interrupting the flow of what you are doing, and without particularly looking at the child.

As a reminder of the lesson expectations, the closer you are to the pupil, the more effective the reminder. Gently approaching the pupil also carries the message that you are certainly not anxious about the situation, even that you feel positive about him, but touching him can too easily be misinterpreted.

## Invalidation of the misbehaviour

- Help the pupil with work making no reference to the misbehaviour.
- Ask a question about work.
- Offer to help the pupil with work in two minutes, and be very sure to give the help within the time.
- Move the pupil for the purpose of work, 'Come and look at this'.
- Change the pupil's work.
- Limit the pupil's choices as to what work he will do next.

A large proportion of low-level disruption, whatever its form, stems from a pupil having difficulty with work. By responding to that underlying problem, the misbehaviour itself is invalidated, and re-defined to the pupil. This re-definition can apply even if the assumption (that work was the underlying problem) is wrong. The classroom agenda, placing work at the head is re-stated and reinforced. By offering or giving help you acknowledge that individuals may need support, and so achieve an element of personal recognition of pupils.

## Praise

Find something to praise in the pupil's work; almost anything will do but make it genuine.

Praise re-defines the misbehaviour into work terms, it invalidates the behaviour element, and also reduces underlying anxiety the pupil may have that he is unable to do the work. Praise must be given privately if it is to be seen as genuine.

## Non-work comment

Refer to the pupil's outside interests, for instance 'Did you get your BMX fixed?'.

If it appears that the pupil's frustration with work cannot be reduced with the preceding techniques, it may be that a brief social interval will help. Initiating that interval can enable you to keep it within bounds. After a fairly brief chat, move the pupil back to the work. This re-establishes that both you and the pupil are human, so the subsequent re-alignment of the pupil to work appears less objectionable. Resolving social anxieties in the pupil may often be a pre-requisite of getting him back to work.

## Defusing the disruption

> Join in the laughter at the disruptive game, then draw it to a halt.

If disruption has escalated into being a social game with a number of pupils involved, a direct confrontation with the group is liable to produce a group response, and that can be serious. By *briefly* accepting that the game is fun, the teacher can acknowledge that element, and avoid alienating and consolidating the group which would result from interpreting their behaviour as an outlawed personal affront. When it comes to moving them back to work, most will respond, and it is possible to help the originators of the disruption who are probably having other difficulties.

## Correcting a confusion

> Give a clear authoritative ruling on the object of pupil-pupil squabbles. For instance: 'That compass is to be shared by the whole of the group'.

Where a minor argument or squabble seems to be developing it is often over some item or other. A straightforward statement can often resolve it. Alternatively, the problem can be defused by providing a spare ruler, book, pair of scissors or whatever. Both of these clearly carry the meaning that the achievement of the set work is by far the most important thing.

> As a follow-up it is worth asking 'Can you two work together now, or should one of you move?'. This throws the responsibility back onto the pupils, and stops them being able to blame the teacher for their plight.

These relatively low-level interventions are summarised in **Figure 9.3.**

## b) Serious problems

If a serious problem occurs, it will be hot and nasty, and will destroy the classroom atmosphere. You must deal with it quickly. Above all you must deal with it in a way that will reduce the heat rather than stoke the fire.

Interventions aimed at controlling low level problems generally acknowledge the inter-personal element, but stress the work aspects of the classroom. Serious problems are always predominantly interpersonal conflicts. For this reason they cannot be resolved with any technique aimed at steering the pupil towards work. The social problem has to be resolved first. This is further emphasised by the fact that a teacher's attempt to move the pupil to work involves the pupil in personal interaction with the teacher, so the social problem arises out of the attempt. Any pupil able to submerge problems of relating to people by working will not be involved in serious

**Figure 9.3**
Intervention tactics for low-level problems

| Intervention technique | Teacher action | Constraints/comments |
|---|---|---|
| **Non-verbal techniques** | Gesture. Just look at the pupil and shake your head, wag a finger or point at the work. | This should be done without anger. |
|  | Get near the pupil. Do this gently, slowly and without interrupting the flow of what you are doing, and without particularly looking at the child. | You can now talk more quietly and show that you know what is going on, that it is less important than work, and that you are not frightened. |
| **Ignore/ invalidate behaviour** | Help the pupil with work making no reference to the misbehaviour. | These are applicable to fairly low-level pupil:peer disruption and they put the misbehaviour in its place as irrelevant as compared with work, without debasing the child. |
|  | Ask questions about work. |  |
|  | Offer to help the pupil with work in 2 minutes, and be very sure to give the help within the time. |  |
|  | Move the pupil for the purpose of work. 'Come and look at this'. |  |
|  | Change the pupil's work. |  |
|  | Limit the pupil's choices as to what work he will do next. |  |
| **Reduce work-based anxiety** | Praise. Find something to praise in the pupil's work, almost anything will do but make it genuine. | Given in private, this emphasises the importance of work and reduces the pupil's anxiety about supposed inability. |
| **Non-work comments** | Involvement in interest. 'Did you get your BMX fixed?'. | This reminds the pupil that you are human and non-aggressive. After a while you can move him on to work. |
| **Defusing the disruption** | Join in the laughter at the disruptive game, then draw it to a halt. | This stops the game being anti-teacher, and reduces group support. |
| **Correct a confusion** | 'That ruler is to be shared by the whole of this group'. | Particularly useful for pupil:pupil problems. |

disruption so the teacher knows that when confronted with serious disruption the predominant conflict is in the personal area.

Such problems are essentially of three types (see Chapter 6 for ideas on the types of disruptive behaviour).

1. **Pupil-pupil problems.** At a serious level this means fighting.
2. **Pupil-teacher problems.** This is a direct confrontation between a pupil and the teacher.
3. **Out of context problems.** This is generally the pupil who is so angry with a teacher, the school, the police or adults in general and you as a representative of all that get in the firing line. (See Chapter 5 for more about the origin of such problems.)

In dealing with such a problem, the first task is to work out which of these applies. There are then other points to clarify in your mind.

Remind yourself of the back-up that is available; where can you call on help. That in itself can be reassuring, and the calmer you are the less the problem is likely to get inflamed. Remember your role is as an adult and it is your responsibility to help all those involved by sorting out the trouble. It is no loss of face to call for help; it is far more important to resolve the problem.

Be objective. The one second delay while you assess the situation is time well spent. Look at it in three ways:
1. What caused the flare up?
2. What is actually happening?
3. What do you want to happen?

## Pupil-pupil conflicts

Remind yourself whether the two involved are regular enemies, or is it unusual for them to be so irate. The rest of the class will probably have told you already if they are always at each other's throats, in which case there is no way to remove the root cause of the battle. You have simply got to separate them.

Move towards the pupils talking quietly but firmly recognising that they are enemies. 'You two obviously can't stand each other, so keep apart. One over there, the other there, and you can avoid this sort of thing. If you want to fight do it during break, this is not the time or place'.

If they are not regular enemies, remind them of the fact. 'What is this about? You two can usually be trusted to get on OK. What are you fighting about?'.

By asking questions you are starting to take control, but you must do more. A firm authoritative decision about the stated cause of the fight can re-establish your position.

Above all do not back away since this shows that you are frightened. But do not get physically involved.

If you need to restrain physically, get help first. (It is worth remembering that it is very rare that such measures are needed.)

Obviously you want the fighting to stop, but if you set yourself the goal of resolving all the underlying conflicts between the pair, you are heading for trouble. You cannot solve the problems of the universe, they go back a long way. You need a settled class, so a truce is often all you can aim at. However you can help, particularly by taking the protagonists seriously, and offering to help resolve arguments if they are prepared to discuss reasonably. However 'now is not the time to sort this out in detail'.

Find a time and opportunity to discuss things with them individually before the next lesson. Watch them both outside your lesson to see how they behave, and take preventative measures next lesson. For instance organise groups differently, find some reason to do more with the two of them. Do not look for trouble next time: prevent it.

If the confrontation is verbal, shouted abuse etc., do not just join in the shouting. Quiet questioning with the odd emphasised word put you in control far better.

Try to separate them. Talk to one of them quietly, turning round if need be to tell the other that you want to see him in just a minute. Then do so. Do not take sides. Do not try to discuss things in front of the class, this is a private matter.

If they continue to shout at each other, try bringing them together, sit down and get them to sit (it's hard to fight sitting, and psychologically hard to hit a sitting person). Then get each in turn to state a case and no more. You are then in command as arbiter. Hang on to the position of control and use it to cut short the shouting.

## Pupil-teacher conflicts

Usually problems here stem from intervention by the teacher in the pupils' activities. So when you interrupt gossiping or other pupil-peer interactions, the pupils can occasionally turn on you. Any form of criticism or threat can generate the problem.

Generally the conflict starts with abuse and insults. This shows as clearly as anything that the child is feeling threatened,and insecure, so shouting, threats and anger from you will make the problem worse.

Move slowly towards the child and you can talk quietly without all the class getting involved. Comments on your parenthood, teaching competence and sexual competence can all be defused with 'Well that is your opinion. We could talk about it some time, perhaps in the head's office or with your parents'. To talk the child down questions like 'Now what has got you so angry?' or 'Could I help you with your work?' can help in that they are related to the problem rather than to the conflict.

Do not touch the child.

You should be as non-threatening as possible. The time for straight domination of the child is long past if you are in a serious confrontation.

As the teacher in the class, you want the pupil to be aware that you are in charge. However direct assertion of authority will seem to be a personal challenge. Being quiet in the face of a storm is a clear statement of authority with no challenge.

You need the child to back down from the challenge that he has issued. He cannot do so in front of his classmates, so reduce the audience size.

Get near him. Quietly reflect to him that 'I seem to have annoyed you, what exactly is it you want?'. And when a quieter moment does arise a clear restatement of the rules of the class can do more than all the shouted commands.

### Out of context trouble

Often you will have no clue as to the origin of the problem, but try to work out when in the lesson trouble broke out. If it was at the very beginning a fair guess is that it was caused by the previous lesson, or at home.

Ask what the problem is.

That doesn't mean that you are committed to solving it, in fact it is reasonable to demand that the pupil's behaviour improves before you can discuss it. 'You settle down now and I can see if there is anything I can do to help you'. Do not commit yourself to the child's point of view. You cannot take on the role of championing his cause, but in some cases you can be an honest broker. To take his problem seriously by offering to listen to him, can defuse the anger a lot.

This kind of angry child is looking for support, and will be just as happy to get it from others in the class as from you. You must make sure that does not happen, but do not compromise your position. You can offer him support, and make clear that you are expecting decent behaviour as a precondition for your help. 'Yes you can go to see the deputy head ... in fact I will go with you at the end of this lesson to help you sort this out, but now let me get the rest of the class started on their work, then I can help you with yours'.

You do not want to join the pupils gang against the deputy head. You want it clear that the classroom is for working in. But you must make it clear that you are interested in the children's well-being also. So your classroom is not the place for this sort of thing.

# 9.4 Conclusions

All the intervention techniques described above have two features in common:

**1.** They are all intended to prevent, reduce or reverse escalation.
**2.** They are intended to get the class back to work.

Often successful intervention involves the teacher in restraining his or her own anger and frustration since that would be counter-productive, fuelling the escalation. However it is well worth while doing this, since it makes such a contribution to a successful classroom.

# Implications for the whole school

In the preceding chapters classroom disruption has been discussed and analysed at some length, and a series of recommendations have been drawn from the analysis. Those recommendations have focussed on the classroom teacher, and what can be done to reduce the problem of disruption at the classroom level. However there are also wider implications that effect the whole school. The wider issues of providing for pupils' needs are the central topic of another title in this series, but there are specific points in relation to behaviour problems.

## 10.1  Teacher differences

Although the behaviour of the teacher in a class is of paramount importance in determining the behaviour of pupil behaviour in that class, it must be remembered that there is a considerable knock-on effect from one lesson to the next. At the crisis level, this can mean that a pupil comes into a lesson having had a serious confrontation with his previous teacher. This can be a source of serious trouble, and was discussed in Chapter 9.

At the more insidious level, major differences in teacher's styles can have an important effect on all concerned. So the liberal teacher working with strict disciplinarian colleagues is likely to have a very hard time. Pupils coming from an authoritarian regime are unlikely to respect, or perhaps even notice the teacher's comments. The other teachers are liable to find fault with the liberal teacher in that pupils leave lessons with him or her out of line with expected behaviour.

The danger is that, throughout a school the style of lesson control can become regulated by these conflicts between staff. Schools need an element of cohesion and unanimity if such stresses are to be reduced. This clearly brings the topic into the area of school management. It has to be the responsibility of senior staff to prevent confrontational classroom control from becoming the school norm. It is hard for individual teachers to move away from such a regime towards more productive relationships with their classes.

## 10.2  Training in classroom control

One of the most effective ways to influence the style of classroom control in a school is by discussion and training. Work with teachers (Kent, 1986) showed that they were very keen to be involved in in-service training on the topic. They valued very highly discussions on ideas and techniques such as those described in this book.

Such discussions clearly must be well structured and organised to take it beyond the mere swapping of staff-room gossip, characterised in Chapter 1. The content of this book as a basis for such work, and the bibliography provides a reading list for those who wish to follow up topics.

## 10.3  Lesson observation

One of the major elements in understanding disruption as discussed in this book is lesson observation. This cannot be the observation that a teacher does while teaching. It is very revealing to watch lessons being taught by other teachers. During training courses this is usually possible, but few practising teachers have the opportunity to watch other people's lessons. Providing the chance and the climate for that could be a major contribution to the training of staff in lesson control.

Methods of observation were discussed and described in Chapter 6. Making time for it is the challenge to teachers, schools and education authorities.

## 10.4  Classroom support

The need for teachers to familiarise themselves with existing support provisions was emphasised in Chapter 7. It is also important to stress the need for such support to exist.

At its most local level support may be best in terms of relatively informal agreements between staff. These may be staff within the same department or staff who happen to work in nearby rooms who agree to relieve pressure if asked. More formal arrangements can be effective, particularly the use of classroom assistants or special needs staff to support the classroom teacher with pupils whose special needs are reflected in their behavioural problems. Whichever way such agreements are arranged, senior staff can contribute considerably by involving themselves in them. Importantly, these agreements are likely to be most effective if they are set up as being reciprocal. It would be a considerable boost to the self-esteem of a new or junior member of staff to be invited to support a head of department, and the reciprocity of the accord would make it even more supportive.

At a whole school level, 'sanctuary', 'time-out rooms' or 'behavioural units' are becoming well established. If a pupil does become out of control the situation can be considerably defused if there is some such long-stop. Sanctuary may be provided by a special needs department. A behavioural unit can operate on a withdrawl basis to provide a different curriculum. Perhaps more importantly it can provide small group teaching for pupils whose behaviour dictates that, as a prerequisite to learning, their personal or social anxiety be allowed for. A time-out room is essentially a place for pupils to cool off, away from the heat of a classroom confrontation. It has to be supervised, but above all going there has to be non-punitive.

These, and other such school based support systems are discussed by Topping (1983), who concludes, above all, that whole school support is extremely valuable. These different forms of provision are also discussed in detail in another volume in the present series.

In addition to these school based forms of support, it is important for teachers to be aware of the additional support available from the authority.

This may include back-up from the Educational Psychologist or Special Needs Adviser, or contact with staff from other special units or special schools. Generally these are only accessible through the hierachy of the school, so contact with senior staff has to be seen as the first step towards the gathering of such help.

# 10.5  Timetables and school organisation

There are numerous constraints on the beleaguered teacher who has to draw up a school time-table. However it may be useful to outline some of the probable effects on pupil behaviour of different systems that may be used.

The now traditional secondary school time-table is based largely on the academic aspect of the classroom agenda (see Chapter 7). The pupils move between lessons to the different rooms where they are taught the range of subjects. They are usually in different groups of pupils for consecutive lessons, in different places with different teachers.

In addition, the reason, the purpose behind all these changes is the teaching of a series of different academic subjects.

For a pupil who finds it hard to relate to adults, this continual switching of teachers must be a strain. For the pupil who has a low academic self-esteem the underlying academic purpose of all the change must be constantly reminding him of his self-perceived handicap. From the point of view of such a pupil, it would be hard to design a more stressful regime. In time-tabling, it would be wise to bear in mind the likely effects of such stress, particularly in terms of it generating disruptive behaviour.

The alternative to the type of time-table described would be for the pupils to remain in one place. In the extreme case the class would then be taught by just one or two teachers. This would value highly the social element of the classroom agenda, and it is worth noting that most primary schools and special schools for behaviour problem pupils adopt such a regime. However for normal secondary schools, this would devalue the academic work that is the other element of the classroom agenda, and that would be a comparable risk.

The problem with the practical solution usually reached is that not only the pupils but also the teachers move from lesson to lesson. With nobody feeling settled, there is a real danger that pupils and teachers are all in a state of considerable stress.

Clearly the time-table has to be a reflection of a compromise reached between the demands of the academic and the social elements of the agenda. However, where behaviour problems are a major chronic problem, they in themselves devalue the work element of the agenda, so have to be resolved as a matter of priority. In such a situation a strong case could be made for modifying the time-table to reduce the inherent stresses of repeated change.

# Conclusion

Classroom disruption is a major problem in schools and this book has focused on the part that teachers themselves can play in reducing the problem, so that the normal positive elements of school can flourish. But although teachers can do a great deal to reduce the problem, it must not be concluded that the fault is theirs entirely or that the responsibility for solving underlying problems is theirs entirely. There are numerous factors that contribute to the generation of disruptive behaviour (see Chapter 2) and many of these are outside the school.

The frequent implication that schools are an effective front-line weapon for dealing with any and every social problem has put an impossible burden onto teachers. Teachers can make a considerable impact on problems in school, but these problems often reflect larger external conflicts, and teachers are ill-advised to try to resolve them, especially if doing so deflects them from their central tasks in school.

# Summary

## Models of teaching

The practical ideas suggested in the second part of this book can, to an extent, be summarised by considering two models of teaching. These are shown in the form of flow-diagrams in Figures 11.1 and 11.2. Neither should be taken too literally, but they serve as a reminder of the points we have made.

In the *first* model, the teacher has planned a lesson without having (or taking into account) the necessary background information. On finding a behaviour problem, the response to it is to use an intervention technique, and if the problem persists to *use the same technique again.* Notice that no direct assessment of the problem is made, no additional background information is used and in the light of the failure of the selected technique, it is not reviewed.

This model is unlikely to be successful. An intervention has to be selected so as to correspond to the situation, and if an intervention has failed to work once it is not likely to succeed a second time, but both pupil and teacher are liable to become more anxious: a problem which probably underlies the failure of the teacher in the first place.

The *second* model of teaching involves the kind of procedure which should underlie your practice and the handling of behaviour problems.

The first step is to plan the lesson in the light of the necessary information.

Once the lesson is under way, it is essential to monitor the class all the time. This is represented by the *scanning loop* checking for behaviour problems: on finding none, you can return to teaching. However on finding a problem, you must first *analyse the nature of that problem.* This involves the use of information from two sources, observation of the class, and the background information previously gathered.

In the light of this analysis you select an intervention technique, and apply it.

If this intervention is successful, you *review the teaching strategy* in the light of the fact that there is a certain amount of disruption, and that may be a criticism of the lesson. In this way there is an element of *continuous monitoring* in your lessons.

If the first intervention is *not* successful, you add that fact to information available in selecting a new intervention technique to try. In other words you *modify your intervention in the light of your new assessment.*

Once again, when the control tactic is successful, you review your teaching strategy. This *reflexive teaching* is a major feature of this second model. It represents *continuous self-monitoring*.

Another important aspect of this second model is that *background information* assumes its rightful place, which is not the case in the first model. This information will be about the pupils, intervention techniques and the back-up that is available to you. This will be collected by observing the pupils, by reference to records and by talking to other teachers about these and other difficulties.

Model 2 is an experimental model of teaching. You try things out, you observe their effect and modify your actions as a result of your observations. It is first and foremost a *model of thoughtful teaching*. A thoughtful teaching model like this does not only apply to the management of disruption or to classroom control, but to all aspects of teaching.

Sometimes Model 2 can be applied in 'real time' in the classroom. Sometimes the assessment and subsequent modification of your teaching will take place between one lesson with a class and the next. In either situation, it is a model which will help you to be more responsive to your pupils' needs.

**Figure 11.1**
Unsuccessful teaching

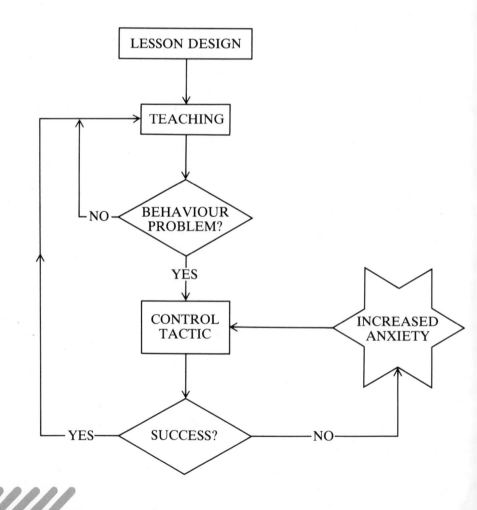

**Figure 11.2**
Successful, reflective teaching

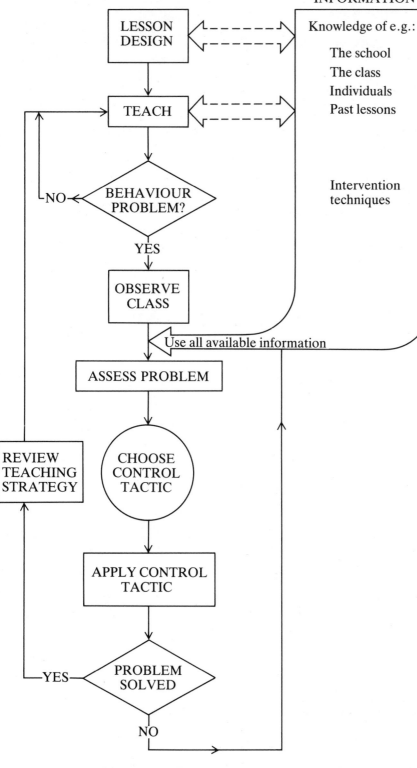

BACKGROUND
INFORMATION

Knowledge of e.g.:

The school
The class
Individuals
Past lessons

Intervention
techniques

LESSON
DESIGN

TEACH

BEHAVIOUR
PROBLEM?

NO

YES

OBSERVE
CLASS

Use all available information

ASSESS PROBLEM

REVIEW
TEACHING
STRATEGY

CHOOSE
CONTROL
TACTIC

APPLY CONTROL
TACTIC

YES

PROBLEM
SOLVED

NO

# Bibliography

Argyle M., 1978, *The Psychology of Interpersonal Behaviour*, Penguin.

Bird C., Cressum R., Furlong J. and Johnson D. (eds), 1980, *Disaffected Pupils*, Brunel University Educational Studies Unit.

Brophy J.E. and Evertson C., 1976, *Learning from Teaching*, Allyn and Bacon.

Cox T., (1977), 'The nature and management of stress in schools', in *The Management of Stress in Schools, Education Department Conference Report*, Clywd County Council, Mold.

Dawson R.L., 1980, *Special provision for disturbed pupil: a survey*, Macmillan Education, Basingstoke.

Dawson R.L., 1982, 'What concerns teachers about their pupils', *Journal of the Association of Educational Psychologists*, 8, pp. 37–40.

Dierenfield, 1982, *Times Education Supplement*.

Farrington D., 1978, 'The family backgrounds of aggressive youths', in Hersor L.A. and Berger M. (eds), *Aggression and antisocial behaviour in childhood and adolescence*, Pergamon, Oxford.

Flanders N.A., 1970, *Analysing teaching behaviour*, Addison-Wesley, Reading, Mass.

Frude N., 1984, 'Frameworks for analysis', in Frude N. and Gault H. (eds), *Disruptive behaviour in schools*, Wiley, Chichester.

Galloway D.M., 1980, 'Exclusions and supervision from school', in *Trends in Education*, 2, pp. 33–8.

Galloway D.M., Bell T., Blomfield D., Seyd R., 1982, *Schools and disruptive behaviour*, Longman, London.

Gannaway H., 1976, 'Making sense of school', in Stubbs and Delamont (eds), *Explorations in Classroom Observations*, John Wiley and Sons, London.

Gnagey W.J., 1970, *The psychology of discipline in the classroom*, Macmillan, London.

Graham P., Rutter M., 1968, 'Organic brain dysfunction and child psychiatric disorder', *British Medical Journal*, 3, pp. 695–700.

Gray J.R., 1987, 'Social Skills and Classroom Disruption', D. Phil Thesis, Oxford University (in prep.).

Gray J.R., Howarth R., Richer J.M., 1986, 'Disruptive Behaviour in School', in Macfarlane A. (ed), *Progress in Child Health*, Vol. 3, Churchill Livingstone (in press), London.

Hargreaves D., 1967, *Social Relations in a Secondary School*, Routledge and Kegan Paul, London.

**84**

Hargreaves D., Hester S.K., Mellor F.J., 1975, *Deviance in classrooms,* Routledge and Kegan Paul, London.

Hinde R., 1970, *Animal Behaviour,* McGraw-Hill, New York.

Hollander E.P., 1978, *Leadership Dynamics, a practical guide to effective relationships,* The Free Press, New York.

Howarth R., 1985, 'A comparison of three methods of investigating social structure in the classroom', Unpublished Thesis for Special Diploma in Educational Studies, University of Oxford.

Kelly H.H. and Michela J.L., 1980, 'Attribution Theory and Research', *Annual Review of Psychology.*

Kent M., 1986, 'The development and evaluation of an in-service training course on classroom control', Unpublished Thesis for Special Diploma in Educational Studies, University of Oxford.

Kounin J.S., 1970, *Discipline and Group Management in Classrooms,* Holt, New York.

Laslett and Smith, 1984, *Effective Classroom Management, A Teacher Guide,* Croom Helm, Beckenham, Kent.

Lawrence J., Steed D., Young P., 1984, *Disruptive children – disruptive schools?,* Croom Helm, London.

Marland M., 1975, *The Craft of the Classroom,* Heinemann, London.

McNamara D., 1975, 'Distribution and incidence of Problem Children in an English County', Paper presented to British Association (paper L251).

Marsh P., Rosser E., Harre R., 1978, *The rules of disorder,* Routledge and Kegan Paul, London.

Pik R., 1981, 'Confrontation situations and teacher-support systems,' in Gillham B. (ed), *Problem Behaviour in Secondary School,* Croom Helm, London.

Power M.J., 1972. 'Neighbourhood schools and juveniles before the courts,' *British Journal of Criminology,* 12, pp. 111–32.

Power M.J., Alderson M.R., Phillipson C.M., Schoenberg E., Morris J.N., 1967, 'Delinquent schools', *New Society,* 19 October.

Raven J., 1978, 'School rejection and its amelioration', *Educational Research,* 20, 3–9.

Rutter M., Tyard J., Whitmore K., 1970, *Health Education and Behaviour,* Longman, London.

Rutter M., Cox A., Tupling C., Berger M., Yule W., 1975, 'Attainment and adjustment in two geographical areas: 1 – Prevalence of psychiatric disorder', *British Journal of Psychiatry, 126,* p 493–509.

Rutter M., Mauchan B., Mortemore P., Custon J., 1979, *Fifteen thousand hours,* Open Books, London.

Shepherd M., Oppenheim B., Mitchell S., 1971, *Childhood behaviour and mental health,* University of London Press, London.

Sturge C., 1982, 'Reading retardation and anti-social behaviour', *Journal of Child Psychology and Psychiatry,* 23,1, 21–31.

Sylva K., Roy C., Painter M., 1980, *Childwatching at Playgroup and Nursery School,* Grant McIntyre, London.

Tattum D., 1982, *Disruptive Pupils in Schools and Units,* Wiley, Chichester.

Thomas A., Chess S., Birch H.G., 1968, *Temperament and Behaviour Disorders in Children,* New York University Press, New York.

Tinbergen N., 1952, '"Derived" activities, their causation, biological significance, origin and emancipation during evolution', *The Quarterly Review of Biology,* 27, 1–32.

Topping K., 1983, *Educational Systems for Disruptive Adolescents,* Croom Helm, Beckenham, Kent.

Trower P., Bryant B., Argyle M., 1978, *Social Skills and Mental Health,* Methuen, London.

Wood D., 1980, *Working with the under-fives,* Grant McIntyre, London.

Yule W., Nerger M., Wigley V., 1984, 'Behaviour modification and classroom management' in Frude N. and Gault H. (eds), *Disruptive Behaviour in Schools,* Wiley, Chichester.

# Notes for tutors

## Introduction

This book was written so as to constitute an introduction to the subject of classroom control, and is designed for 'remote learning': for students working on their own trying to improve their skills and understanding of classroom dynamics. In this context, the word 'Student' is used for any teacher who is studying the topic, not exclusively for pre-service student-teachers. Where such students have the good fortune to be working on this topic *with* a tutor, it is possible to adapt and enhance the outline of the book. In this case, the sequence in which ideas are introduced may profitably be altered, and some additional elements may also be introduced.

## The existing text

The outline of the existing text is summarised below. There are four principal elements to it, and their aims are as follows:

**1.** Background information on the subject of classroom disruption (Chapters 1–3). This was introduced at the beginning of the book so as to give students with little or no experience of classrooms some facts to work on.

**2.** A theoretical framework with which to think about the subject of classroom disruption, both in terms of the causes of the phenomenon, and the teacher's intervention (Chapters 4–5). This theoretical understanding is seen as essential to improving teachers' skills in classroom control.

**3.** Some suggestions for the investigation of classroom disruption (Chapter 6). These are intended to enable students to test the ideas outlined in the previous section, and so increase their understanding of the phenomenon.

**4.** Recommendations (Chapters 7–10). These 'tips for teachers' are deliberately based on the theoretical frameworks developed above. Without this, they would be seen as anecdotal and unfounded.

Tutors will note that the sequence above is designed for students with little or no experience of classrooms, and with little access to schools. However, it is possible to adapt this set of elements to suit other specific situations, and groups of 'students'. Suggestions for doing so are made below, and are laid out for different groups of students.

# Video

One general suggestion may be made, and that is to encourage the use of video recordings in work on classroom control. One of the problems that tutors have in discussing the entire topic, and especially in discussing control methods, is that descriptions of such methods always appear rather limp. By obtaining recordings of real teachers working with real pupils, it is possible to show students the behaviour of pupils, and exact examples of control skills in a context that is self-evidently genuine. Such recordings are of great value.

It is even possible to go further and record students themselves working with classes. These recordings can open up discussion with those students even better. However, it is important not to forget that such recordings can be very threatening to students, and they are generally best discussed with individuals privately.

The very best way to get over these problems is for the tutor to have recordings made of his or her own teaching. These recordings can then be used in discussion with the group, and serve the double purpose of demonstrating control tactics in practice, and of showing that classroom control skills are universally applicable.

# Specific situations

## Pre-service students with access to schools

Where students have good access to schools, but little experience of the classroom, their situation is decidedly better than that envisaged in the writing of the book. Regular access to schools as an observer makes it possible for a student to use direct observation, and personal experience in coming to an understanding of the theoretical framework of classroom behaviour. This is clearly to be preferred to providing the student with theoretical ideas. For this reason, it is suggested that tutors may be able to combine the two elements of 'background information' (part **1** above) and 'investigation' (part **3** above) to make up the initial part of the course.

From this information base it will be possible for the tutor to help students to derive, and therefore to understand the theoretical framework of the phenomenon of disruption.

## Pre-service students on school-based courses

Where students are on school-based courses, the use of the book can be extended considerably. In this case, three elements comprise the initial part of the course in classroom control.

The lecture-based element constitutes the background information (part **1**). This can usefully be combined with practical work in Chapter 7 (from part **4**) which contains suggestions for students to gather information about classes, pupils and lessons. Add to this the observation suggestions (part **3** above) and the student will be able to learn a great deal about the background to classroom disruption and classroom control. These three elements together constitute the ideal background to a student's understanding of the phenomenon of classroom disruption and control.

Follow-up work can introduce the theoretical ideas that make up part **2** of the book, and this can illuminate subsequent observation, as well as forming the basis for the students' own teaching. In this way, the recommendations that constitute part **4** can then form the basis both for the students' actual teaching, and also for the tutor's discussions with students of that teaching. In that latter task, the tutor's attention is particularly drawn to the points made at the beginning of Chapter 8 about the need for the teacher to strike a balance between work and social contact with pupils. This can constitute a very useful basis for objective discussion of lessons with students who have a basic understanding of the process of classroom control.

## In-service work with practising teachers

Where a tutor is working with practising teachers, two new considerations come to the fore. The first is the anxiety of the students about their own competence. This is discussed in the book in Chapters 4 and 10, but must not be underestimated. Allaying the students' fears becomes a prime consideration in working with practising teachers.

The second consideration is that teachers who are in-post generally have little opportunity for lesson observation. As was stressed in Chapter 4, observation of one's own lesson is not a substitute for the detached observation of other teachers at work.

If work with practising teachers is really brief, a short lecture or two, the best use of this book is to base the work on parts **1** and **2** followed by brief reference to part **4**. In this way it is possible to give the 'students' something of a new theoretical understanding of the problem, from which they can develop their own practice. It is however very important to start with the material in Chapter 1 ('How big is the problem?') so as to allay fears of personal incompetence.

If there is more time, it is suggested that the tutor can concentrate more on strengths of members of the group, and base work more on discussion rather than lectures. Where possible, members should be encouraged to make arrangements to observe lessons taught by other teachers (part **3**), since this can provide essential material for the discussion of the topic. Where this is really not possible, video recordings of lessons can offer something of a substitute. In either case, discussion is best focused on the theoretical understanding of the problem (part **2**): practising teachers are generally able to flesh out that understanding with specific recommendations (part **4**) from their own experience.

# Index